Because of You, I Am

. . . .

A *Spiritual Quest with*
Man's Best Friend

MARY ANN BUMBERA

TURNING
STONE
PRESS

First published in 2013 by
Turning Stone Press, an imprint of
Red Wheel/Weiser, LLC
With offices at:
665 Third Street, Suite 400
San Francisco, CA 94107
www.redwheelweiser.com

The names of some people and animals have been changed to
protect privacy.

ISBN: 978-1-61852-076-0

Cover design by Jim Warner
Cover image: Jennifer Mordini

Printed in the United States of America
10 9 8 7 6 5 4 3 2 1

For my boys

Contents

Acknowledgments

To the person who taught me to "listen to my gut" and who made this story possible by gifting me with Charlie and Toby—my mother. I am eternally grateful.

To my beloved friend and teacher of life, Ishwar. Without you, this book would not exist. Your constant encouragement to relay my most profound experiences just as they happened sustained me to write every word. The spiritual foundation you gave me allowed me to understand my insights so they could blossom into deeper meaning. No words exist to express my love, admiration, and gratitude.

To my friend Carol Glegg, who toiled in helping me with edits and never for a moment wavered in her belief that this story needed to be told.

To some of the most talented writers I know, the ladies of my writing critique group: Sara Shacter, Ruth Spiro, Sarah Roggio, Beverly Patt, Jude Mandel, Beverly Spooner, and Marlene Hill Donnelly. Somehow, through mountains of popcorn, Bev P.'s luscious lemon squares, countless bad puns, and hoots of laughter, I honed my writing skills. I owe you a gazillion thanks for your critiques and support.

To Steve, for his steadfast encouragement to "stay the course!"

To Penelope Smith, who opened me to a whole new world. I am grateful for your friendship and guidance.

To Linda Kohanov, who by example and a few simple words, inspired me to write the way she writes and lives—authentically.

And to Toby, my Little Shaman Boy, who amazed and uplifted me with his healing powers.

Today, more than ever before, life must be characterized by a sense of Universal responsibility, not only nation to nation and human to human, but also human to other forms of life.

—His Holiness the Dalai Lama

Prologue

When I was twelve years old my miniature poodle, Daisy, died. Six months later, my grandmother died. I remember my brother's accusatory voice saying, "You cried more for Daisy than you did for Grandma!"

It was true. Though I had dearly loved my doting grandma, the truth was that the loss of Daisy, my loving companion and best friend, left a bigger hole in my heart and life. At the time, my brother's indignation left me feeling guilty, as though the depth of my love for Daisy was an affront to my grandmother. But as I got older, I came to appreciate the love I felt for Daisy. I realized that it wasn't wrong to love an animal more than a person and that it is equally important to acknowledge grief that is associated with animals. I think it comes down to a simple truth—love is love.

Grieving the death of a loved one—animal or human—is, in my opinion, the most wrenching experience in life. Even if we are fully aware of their impending death, nothing can prepare us for the actual physical loss. One day they are conscious living beings, the next they are not. A shell of a body is left behind and we don't know where their life force or consciousness goes. Do our loved ones still have some sort of awareness? Can they still see us? Are they happy? These are the mysteries of death that compound our grief.

Death and grieving frequently cause people to question the nature of life and wonder whether there is anything more to us than our physical existence. For me, it was the illness of my beloved dog, Charlie, that triggered my pursuit of what lies beyond the physical and spurred my quest for an understanding of what I came to see as the true Divine Self, or Spiritual Essence.

Charlie, a fifty-five-pound black standard poodle, was one of the greatest teachers of my life. He cracked my heart open, changing the course of my life so that I could stop searching for love from other people and find it in what seemed to be the most unlikely place: myself.

As Charlie aged and grew ill, I feared his death so intensely that death became a hated enemy. Adding to my angst was the realization that the concepts I had believed all my life—returning to God, the immortal soul, life everlasting, and reincarnation—no longer provided solace. So I did the only thing I knew to do—I became obsessed with obtaining a deeper spiritual understanding of death. I needed to *know*, not intellectually, but in the depths of my being, what actually happens to our life force or consciousness when we die.

Ultimately, in my search, I discovered that while the searing pain of grief tests our ability to endure, death is by no means an enemy. In understanding death, I came to an awareness of my own spiritual essence in the most profound ways.

∾

I named Charlie after John Steinbeck's dog in his book *Travels with Charley: In Search of America*. Steinbeck's Charley was also a black standard poodle who accompanied him during his 1960s drive through the United States as he sought to connect with the soul of America and its people. Coincidentally (or not), my Charlie took me on a different yet similar kind of quest—one of reconnection with my own soul through Eastern philosophy, animal communication, shamanism, swimming with humpback whales and dolphins, and study of energy healing. This journey gave me insights into the process of death, the nature of the afterlife of both humans and animals, and the nature of life itself. All in all, it was a journey of understanding love.

This is the story of how that journey unfolded for me: in travels with my own dearest Charlie.

Charlie

Alissa Behn/Pet Personalities

Intuition

Tears prickled my eyes.

The compassion in my veterinarian's eyes spoke what she was not saying.

"Am I ready for this?" I asked in a choked whisper.

"I'm sorry," she said softly. "We've found something on Charlie's X-ray."

Her words, gently spoken as they were, slammed into my heart like a razor-sharp javelin. Charlie, my twelve-year-old black standard poodle, was not only the love of my life, but also my best friend, protector, and healer. With no children of my own, he was also a surrogate child. No, I could never be ready for this.

It had all begun a few nights before, when I'd been awakened in the middle of the night by a short, dry cough from Charlie. There was nothing the least bit alarming about the cough itself, as he'd had no previous respiratory health issues. But in the seconds it took me to reach a fully wakeful state, my intuition told me something was wrong. So when I called the veterinary clinic the next morning requesting an appointment for a chest X-ray, I played up the coughing. I knew they wouldn't agree to a chest X-ray simply because Charlie had coughed once in the night.

"Yes, he's had the cough off and on for a couple of weeks now," I lied.

Even though I knew my open-minded vet, Dr. Pat, welcomed intuitions, I suddenly doubted myself and was reluctant to say that I had a hunch something was wrong. I didn't want to look foolish if everything was okay. Hanging up the phone, I wondered just how silly I'd been for making the appointment because of one measly cough. Charlie's recent blood tests had been fine and he showed no other signs of ill health.

As I sat alone in the exam room the next day, waiting for Charlie to be X-rayed, I continued to berate myself, feeling ridiculous for wasting everyone's time.

But when Dr. Pat came in carrying the X-rays in her hand, I saw the heaviness in her face and felt my world start to crumble. After placing Charlie's X-ray on the lighted screen, she pointed to a mass in his right lung.

"Because of the location, it's not possible to biopsy or aspirate with a bronchial scope," she said. "The only way to tell what kind of mass it is, or determine if it's cancerous, is to perform major thoracic surgery, which would not only be hard on Charlie but would be too drastic at this time."

"So . . . what . . . " I searched for words.

"So let's wait," she said with a more hopeful look on her face. "Let's wait a few months and do follow-up X-rays. There aren't any other lung masses present so it may not be cancer. Let's hope for the best."

I prayed it wasn't cancer. I couldn't imagine my life without Charlie. I tried to stay positive. But anguish settled in my heart.

My Charlie Boy

I can't remember a day of my life when my family didn't have a standard poodle—a black standard poodle. Admittedly I'm biased, but I think their intelligence, good nature, and beauty make them an exceptional breed. I have had other breeds—including mixed breeds—and still I love standard poodles the best. Both my mother and I have always preferred the black ones. I don't know why. We just do.

I was well into adulthood and recently married when the bundle of curly black fur, otherwise known as Charlie, came into my life. It was a newspaper ad that had caught my eye. It simply said "standard poodle puppies" and gave a phone number. The mere sight of the words—standard poodle puppies—made my heart squeal with child-like glee. But I was still mourning my standard poodle, Ralph, who had just died, and I decided I wasn't ready. Nevertheless, I couldn't bring myself to throw out the ad and placed it on the kitchen table. For the remainder of the afternoon it was as if the ad had bewitched me; I repeatedly returned to the kitchen to glance at it.

I found myself daydreaming, imagining the puppies jumping in my lap, clamoring for attention. I could almost feel the soft pads of their little feet on my legs, their spongy tongues licking my face with their pungent puppy breath. Needle-sharp teeth nibbled at my hands and feet. And they were, of course, black. But . . . wait a minute . . . what if they *weren't* black? I grabbed the ad and dialed the number.

Eight weeks old, the woman told me.

"What color are they?"

"Black."

I hung up. In record time, my index finger punched in my mother's number.

"Well, are you going to get one?" she asked excitedly.

"I don't know. I'm not sure I'm ready yet."

After hanging up, I curled up on the couch, plunging into grief over Ralph. Would I ever be able to forget that sick feeling in my gut when I signed the paper for the veterinary school to euthanize him? How could I live with the regret of letting the vet talk me out of being with him when they did it? Would I always be haunted by the intense, quizzical look on his face when he turned his head back to me as they wheeled him down the hall to "do the deed"? Who had been with him? Did anyone comfort him or hold him or tell him what was happening? Had he been scared? Had he gone quickly? My only solace, I thought, was that my husband and I had buried him in our backyard.

The peal of the phone nudged me out of my self-reproaching heartache. Wiping my eyes, I picked up the receiver. My mother's jubilant voice rang out.

"Will you go get me one of those puppies?" she said. "I'll get one for you too!"

Her exuberance was so contagious that my heartache faded. A puppy! Suddenly I felt like an elated five-year-old! My mother was going to buy me a *puppy*!

~

A few nights later, my husband and I went to pick out the two puppies. I reveled in the playful little balls of fur tumbling all over me. One of them kept plopping in my lap. Every time I'd put him down to look at the others, PLOP! There he'd be, back again. There was just something special about this persistent, cuddly, sweet little fella who wouldn't leave me alone. And so Charlie entered my life. Little did I know at the time that he would change my life so profoundly.

Charlie instantly became a mamma's boy. His registered American Kennel Club name was Daz L.M. Charles le Chien. And dazzle 'em he did! Even as a young dog, Charlie's regal presence was noticed by passersby. "Beautiful dog!" people called out everywhere we went. My response was always, "Thank you! He thinks so too!" Charlie accepted these compliments like a title rightly due him and would puff out his chest, with head and tail held high, and strut with an air of sophistication that said, "You think that's beautiful? Well check this out!"

My mom with our first standard poodle, Cleopatra. In mom's lap is our miniature poodle, Daisy

Me as a child with one
of our poodle puppies

Me with Charlie and his
littermate shortly after
bringing them home

One of my favorite, unique traits about Charlie
was that he loved to brush his own teeth. As a puppy,
I let him gnaw on his toothbrush in hopes of getting him accustomed to it. This plan worked too well.
Surprisingly enough, the beef-flavored toothpaste wasn't

Charlie's first snow at four months old. Throughout his life, he loved snow—especially eating it

the attraction. It was the bristles. Before bed, he would paw at the bathroom cupboard where his toothbrush was kept. I would squeeze out the toothpaste, put the toothbrush on the floor, and Charlie would step on the handle to steady it and ever so gently crunch the bristles. And crunch. And crunch. If I didn't take it away after a minute, he'd have kept crunching until the bristles were gone. And just as any English gentleman knows the proper teatime, Charlie considered bedtime the only proper time at which to brush his teeth. If his toothbrush was offered at any other time of day, he refused. Unless, of course, a houseguest accidentally left his or her toiletry bag open—then their toothbrush was fair game, no matter what hour of day!

As a young adult dog, one of Charlie's trademarks was how he said hello to people. Despite our attempt at training, he stood firm in his belief that the only appropriate salutation for people was to kiss them on the mouth. If we didn't grab him in time, he'd be leaping in the face of some poor unsuspecting guest, startling them with a slob-bery kiss. Good thing he brushed his teeth!

Whenever we returned home from a trip, Charlie would stand indignantly by the suitcases, waiting for us to open them. The instant they were unzipped, his head disappeared inside. With the precision of Sherlock Holmes investigating a crime scene, he nosed out the details of our leave of absence. This was also the routine for anything brought into the house—from the smallest shopping bag to the toolbox of the furnace repairman. *Anything* that entered his house had to be given his sniff of approval. Long before Homeland Security was neces-sary, Charlie was on the job.

~

Over the course of his life, Charlie taught me innu-merable profound lessons, beginning with one of the toughest—to listen to what my heart says is right. When Charlie was not quite one year old, I wanted to fence the yard so Charlie could run free, but my husband and I couldn't agree on a type of fencing or the cost involved. In a quandary over other possibilities, I allowed the trainer at the dog obedience school to convince me to use a shock collar to teach Charlie the limits of the yard. She said that the electric shock from the hand-held device was not strong enough to hurt Charlie. And besides, she said, wasn't a little shock, similar to ones used in invisible fencing, better than him getting hit by a car or getting lost? I figured she knew better than I, so I did what she suggested. But it felt wrong.

After a few short sessions, Charlie learned to stay inside the yard. It still felt wrong, but I continued because it seemed to be working. Then I followed the trainer's instructions to "reinforce" his learning. She told me to stand just beyond the edge of the yard and call him to me. If he came out of the yard, I was to give him a gentle zap.

When I called Charlie, he sat there, looking extremely puzzled. He was eager to obey me, yet he knew he shouldn't cross the boundary. When I called him a second time, he happily and willingly bounded toward me. His face was beaming with pride when suddenly he crossed the boundary and ZAP! The shock stopped him in his tracks. The confusion and hurt in his eyes instantly told me that I had betrayed his trust. I realized that training him this way would only harm our relationship. Riddled with shame and guilt, I returned the shock collar to the trainer and deeply regretted not following what I knew was right. I vowed to never again give anyone, professional or otherwise, precedence over what my heart told me. So I settled for a fifty-foot cable dog run so that Charlie could at least stretch his legs and chase a few squirrels.

This hard knocks lesson of learning to follow my heart shifted my perspective of animals in general. All my life I had proudly professed being an animal lover. But this experience zapped *me* into realizing the sickening truth—that although I did indeed love animals, my social conditioning had allowed me to look upon them as lesser things—property to be owned, dominated, and controlled. Thus, I had been easily persuaded into a harsh training technique by a bad trainer. I vowed that in the future, I would seek only positive reinforcement training instead of training techniques based on pain and intimidation. From it all, I started to see animals as sentient, individual beings—beings who deserve force-free handling and compassion equal to us humans.

∿

Charlie became my bedrock of emotional support. His loving presence got me through my unhappy marriage and heart-wrenching, though amicable, divorce. In our divorce settlement the question of who would get custody of Charlie was never raised, but I would've relinquished anything to keep him. It was Charlie who got me through that miserable, lonely time, bringing meaning and purpose into my life when I felt I had none. And, being the best cuddler, Charlie always lifted my sprits—no matter what.

Soon after my divorce, I decided to move back to my community of friends in the Chicago area and began my search for a house in the northern suburbs. My criterion for the house was simple: it had to have a manageable fenced-in yard big enough for Charlie to run in, chase squirrels or birds, and call his own. As luck would have it, I found such a yard accompanied by an affordable house that I liked.

∿

Despite Charlie's endearing traits, he was a handful. As smart, loving, gentle, and affectionate as he was, he was fiercely protective of me. Tollbooths were always a challenge with him in the car. When a toll collector reached out his or her hand towards the car, Charlie erupted in a protective frenzy. I became adept at squeezing my arm through a tiny opening in the window to give or get change. As I sped away in embarrassment, he would stop barking and, pivoting to keep the tollbooth in sight, give one last woof of triumph, then curl up and go to sleep.

I reciprocated in my protectiveness towards Charlie. When I bought my home and installed an alarm system, my spiritual mentor, Ishwar, said, "You got Charlie to protect you and an alarm system to protect Charlie." I opened my mouth to rebuff this ridiculous statement but sheepishly realized that, well . . . it was true. I'd just never thought of it that way.

When Charlie was around three years old he became aggressive towards most other dogs, although there were a few he liked. If he deemed a dog as foe, he lunged and barked with the wild ferociousness of a mamma bear protecting her cubs. I couldn't control him at these times and it always took me a while to calm him down. I quickly learned that getting angry and pulling on his leash fueled his frenzy. At the time, positive behavior modification training for dog-reactive dogs wasn't available, or at least I was not aware of it. (Fortunately, it exists today.) Since Charlie wasn't the least bit food-motivated, I relied on other avoidance techniques—such as ushering him in and out the back door at the vet's office. As soon as I saw another dog on our walks, I diverted his attention. Although the avoidance tactics worked, his dog aggression remained a sore spot with me. I hated it when he spun into his barking frenzies and nothing seemed to help him.

Charlie's fierce protectiveness and dog aggression was a mystery to me because he was a quintessential loving, *gentle* dog. What could be the cause of his aggression? Had I waited too long to have him neutered, perhaps? Was I doing something wrong to make him this way? But when I reflected on when the protectiveness and dog aggression had started, I realized that this behavior had magnified enormously after my divorce. I came to understand that because animals are usually so in tune with their people, the intensity of Charlie's protectiveness directly mirrored the degree of my personal safety issues. He was mirroring my deep-seated anxieties about taking care of myself in the scary, "big, bad world." So while I still needed to work with Charlie on this (and also with myself), at least it made some sense to me.

In other ways, too, Charlie's awareness of my emotions touched and surprised me. Whenever I got wound in a tizzy, usually over something trivial, he jumped on me—sometimes even knocked me down—and licked my face over and over until I laughed. Without fail, this made me see that whatever I had been upset about held no importance in the grand scheme of things. And if I had an upsetting phone call, the moment I'd hang up, he'd be there with his head in my lap or to offer a gentle kiss. Initially, I thought the tone of my voice was tipping him off, but I began to see that even if my voice sounded happy, he still always knew when I needed comforting. At first I marveled at this, but later realized the truth of the matter—Charlie was more in tune with me than I was with myself.

∾

One of my favorite photos
of Charlie and me

Charlie was literally my lifesaver. At an exceptionally dark time of my life, within just four months, I suffered a broken engagement, a painful parting of ways with a long-time friend and, worst of all, the death of my best friend. These losses, especially of my best friend, whom I had utterly adored, made my grief unbearable. I pondered suicide. I didn't really want to end my life. I just didn't feel strong enough to endure the searing emotional pain.

One night after returning home from a therapy session that had left me feeling even more depressed and alone, I pulled into the garage and watched the garage door close in my rearview mirror—but did not turn off the ignition. As I sat in the car, wishing that I would die, I thought of Charlie. What would happen to him? Who would take him? Who would cuddle him? Would he be happy without me? It then dawned on me that the carbon monoxide that would kill me could also seep into the house and kill Charlie. I cut the engine.

When I walked in the house, Charlie bounded to greet me. I knelt in the hallway as he performed his

Charlie surprising me with a kiss

exuberant welcome home dance around me. I felt loved, needed, and adored, and tears streamed down my face. I knew that somehow I would make it through this. And it was none other than Charlie who nursed me through the worst of it. Friends, of course, were supportive and helpful, but in the privacy of one's own home the true darkness of pain raises its ugliest head. Charlie never left my side when I wailed and was racked with sobs. Whenever I began to cry, with utmost tenderness, he licked away my countless tears. Through this, he taught me endurance, strength, and self-respect—qualities that finally pulled me back into my life.

Through loving me when I couldn't or didn't know how to love myself, Charlie taught me tenderness and patience in dealing with my emotions. And he showed me that the unconditional love he had for me is how I should love and care for myself. Not easy to do, but he continuously held the example for me.

The Other Man in My Life

Charlie was a thief of many hearts, but there was one other, besides mine, that he stole completely—that of my boyfriend, Steve. But their first introduction didn't go so well.

I barely knew Steve when the law firm handling my grandmother's estate in Ohio appointed Steve to be the family's local liaison. When Steve wasn't on duty as a fire department lieutenant, he worked at the law firm as a paralegal and insurance mediator and investigator.

One summer morning when Charlie and I were at my grandmother's house helping my mom sort through things, Charlie was lying on the floor next to me at the kitchen table when Steve stopped by. The screen door was unlocked and Steve slipped in without knocking, as he was accustomed to doing. What he didn't know this particular time was that there was a one-year-old, fifty-five-pound, very protective poodle beside me. Growling, with teeth bared, Charlie hurled himself at Steve with the undeniable intent of putting this unknown intruder in his place. With Charlie lunging at him, Steve slammed himself against the screen door, where Charlie kept him pinned until I could grab Charlie and reassure him that Steve was on our side.

The next time I saw Steve, he said, "You know, after I met Charlie the other day, I walked back to the office wondering how I, a six-foot-one two-hundred-pound macho man, Vietnam veteran, firefighter, and paramedic, was going to tell my co-workers, fellow firefighters, and Harley biker buddies that I'd been terrorized by a poodle."

"So what did you tell them?" I had to ask.

"I was too chicken to tell 'em! Some things are just better left unsaid!"

The intensity of Charlie and Steve's first meeting would later be matched by the depth of devotion they developed for one another. Over the following year during my Ohio visits, they became fast friends.

Years later, when Steve and I became a couple, I began to understand the thread of their bond when I realized the common denominator they shared—both were big-hearted macho men. Instead of wishing their machismo away, I started to appreciate what they reciprocally gave one another.

When I watched Steve and Charlie mosey on their walks, play ball, or just sit and snuggle, I sensed that for Steve, Charlie provided a brotherly type figure and confidant for all the unexpressed, haunting memories and emotions he had from being a Vietnam veteran and firefighter and paramedic.

"I've never had such comfort, acceptance, or love from an animal before," Steve said once. "Actually, truth be told, from any other person either."

"I understand," I said. I was touched that Charlie could give Steve a comfort he'd never known.

For Charlie, Steve was an outlet for doing "manly" things such as going on long, exploratory walks. Interestingly, Charlie's aggression towards other dogs was less of a problem when Steve walked him without me. It seemed obvious that with Steve, Charlie didn't feel the need to wear his hat of protector.

I often teased Steve that he was like Charlie. Charlie knew he wasn't supposed to bark (like out an open window at someone jogging by at 5:30 AM). I would say to him sternly, "Don't you dare bark!" He would oblige my request and blow his cheeks out, making a loud puffing noise to ensure his effort was duly noted.

"You look just like Charlie when you're mad," I said to Steve once when he was fuming over something. "Only when I tell *you* not to bark, you don't listen!"

"Well, he's had more years of training with you than I have," he said, puffing out his cheeks, imitating Charlie.

Steve's and Charlie's lives also proved to be intertwined in more mysterious ways. And Charlie proved to be someone else's lifesaver. One morning, Steve's 5:30 AM daily departure to a local restaurant for breakfast and coffee was delayed thirty minutes because Charlie uncharacteristically insisted on his walk *before* Steve left instead of when he returned home. This half-hour delay put Steve in the right place at the right time to save the life of a woman in the restaurant who would have choked to death without his intervention. Steve received an award from the mayor and fire chief for this act.

"Well, we both know who the *real* hero is!" I teased Steve.

"Yeah!" he held up the plaque, pointing to the space under his name. "We should've had the mayor put Charlie's name right here!"

Steve's love for Charlie melted my heart. And my relationship with Charlie was further enriched because Steve's delight in him allowed me to appreciate Charlie even more. I told Steve this and he said, "Well, I understand what Charlie has brought to your life. And I've got the utmost respect and admiration for him. I have never expected to step in and replace Charlie's place in your heart. Besides," he said, stifling a laugh, "unless I want to chase strangers down the street or bark at the UPS truck, I'll just let Charlie do what he does best!"

"Well, that's an image I think I can do without!" I laughed.

"And, if push ever comes to shove," he said, "and you have to choose between me or Charlie, I'll voluntarily hop in my truck and mosey on down the road."

"What the heck prompted this?" I asked.

"I don't know. I was just thinking that sometimes in life 'either-or' decisions come up. And the bottom line is that you gotta do what's best for you."

"And?" I asked.

"Well," he said and shrugged his shoulders, "I got an ultimatum once from an ex-girlfriend. She said it was either her or my Harley."

"Let me guess," I said. "You kept the bike."

"Yep!"

Moments of Truth

About a year after I had managed to muster the courage to walk away from an unfulfilling career in corporate America, Charlie's true purpose in my life became clear—to put me on the path of my life's work.

One September day, a friend mentioned that she knew of an animal communicator in the Chicago area by the name of Carol Schultz.

"Animal communicator? What's that?"

"She can talk to animals and hear what they say," Sandy said. "She's giving an introductory workshop at a pet store near here. Want to come?"

Though I was skeptical, a feeling of excitement and intrigue overtook me as I drove to the store the following Saturday.

"The purpose of this work," Carol began, "is to gain deeper insights and awareness of our animal companions—not only to shed light on their behaviors and misbehaviors, but to understand their point of view or what they're feeling. Using honed telepathic skills, we perceive images, intuitive-knowings, concepts, feelings, direct thoughts, or physical sensations. Then we acknowledge these perceptions and translate them into language."

I was riveted. I thought Carol must be some sort of goddess—she could actually *do* this!

"In knowing what our animal friends are thinking and feeling," Carol continued, "we deepen the bond between ourselves and our animals."

"What about communicating with wild animals?" a woman asked.

"The communication is the same. But the beauty of communicating with animals in the wild is that we can relearn to deeply connect with nature and its profound spiritual wisdom."

"Can you communicate with animals who have died?" another woman asked.

"Yes," Carol said. "It's one of the most rewarding aspects of being an animal communicator—to assist someone through their grief and let them know their animal friend is okay." She paused. "So, as I mentioned, animal communicators use telepathy to communicate with animals. Telepathy is the most natural, innate form of communication that exists. In fact, we all use it every day, only we're not aware of it. It is defined as 'feeling at a distance.' Telepathy is how people can get feelings or information from or about other people who are miles away. Have any of you 'known' something about a friend or loved one who was miles away even though you hadn't spoken to them?"

A few hands went up. I wanted to raise my hand but felt too shy.

"But you can also receive telepathic communication from a person standing in front of you," Carol said. "Animal communication works the same way. We can receive information from animals who are right in front of us or miles away. Did everyone bring a photo of an animal friend?"

We all held up our photos.

"Great! So now I'll help you connect with your animals the way animal communicators do. We'll quiet ourselves in a meditation and make a heart-to-heart connection with them. Then you can ask them questions and get information from them. So get comfortable, feel your feet on the floor, and take a few deep breaths."

I wiggled around in my chair to find the comfiest spot. I took some breaths and held Charlie's photo in my lap. I couldn't help but smile at his cute, moustached face looking back at me.

During the meditation, I was able to feel a deep, loving, heart-to-heart connection with Charlie, but that's as far as it went. I didn't feel any physical sensations from him or receive any thoughts or feelings. I enjoyed feeling the connection but was a bit disappointed that I didn't magically receive anything else. Maybe my expectations were too high?

At any rate, everything Carol said about telepathy felt right to me. As I drove home, I remembered that when I was younger, my mother claimed I was psychic because I simply seemed to "know" things about people or events. But throughout my life, I never considered myself particularly gifted in this way. Whenever I "knew" things, I tossed them off as coincidence. Yet I had recently begun to be aware that these "coincidences" were happening more frequently. I knew, for example, when friends— even ones I didn't keep in close contact with—were sad or troubled. And I realized that I "knew" things before people would tell me. Although my mind wavered a bit about the validity of it all, my heart believed that telepathy was authentic.

I scheduled a phone consultation with Carol. My intuition told me that Charlie had some very significant things to convey to me. And there were a few things I was eager to know from him.

Not only was I right, but what Charlie said in our first consultation with Carol set the wheels in motion for what I now realize he'd been preparing me for ever since that first night when he kept plopping so insistently in my lap.

As agreed, I sent Carol my questions for Charlie before the session. All she knew about him was his name, age, breed, and that I'd gotten him as a puppy. She didn't know anything else about our relationship. She assured me that she would get the same information during a phone consultation as she would in meeting Charlie one on one. Even though I believed in telepathy, this was still a small leap of faith.

Minutes before the scheduled consultation time, Steve and I readied ourselves at the dining room table with a pen and notepad.

"Who's going to take the notes?" I asked.

"You take the notes," Steve said. "I'll be the second pair of ears."

"Okay," I said. "Oh, I'm nervous. I don't know what to expect." I looked at Charlie, who was lying beside Steve. "I can't wait to hear what you have to tell us, Baby Boy!" I got on the floor beside Charlie. "This is so weird, isn't it?" I said, looking up at Steve. "I mean, here is Charlie lying here and Carol is going tell us by phone what he's feeling and thinking."

"I'm just glad someone can do it," Steve leaned down to stroke Charlie's head. "So that we know what's going on with this marvelous creature."

Once we'd connected on the phone, Carol said, "Let me take a minute to tune in to Charlie."

Steve and I waited, making silent, silly, kid-like, excited faces at each other.

"Okay," Carol said.

I grabbed my pen.

"The first thing Charlie wants you to know is that on the night you chose him, he says *he* was the one who picked *you*. He says he knew that you were the person who was supposed to take care of him and didn't want you to leave without him."

"Huh," I said. "I always felt that from him. Even on that night."

Already, this session was no longer a leap of faith. I was hooked.

"Okay. Let's get to your questions," Carol said. "I have them here, but go ahead and ask in whatever order you want."

"Well, the one I'm dying to know the answer to is: What does Charlie want me to know about myself?"

"He says, 'Think about it—go within!'"

"Oh my God!" I gasped. "Wow! I *knew* he was going say that." My mind raced to the many messages I'd received lately, everywhere I turned, advising me to look inside myself. There was absolutely no way Carol could have known this.

"Well, he's pretty insistent about it," Carol said. "He says it's time."

"Okay," I said. "Well, I guess I need to listen to him on that one. Does he have any physical ailments I'm not aware of?"

"He says his hips are hurting him," Carol said. "Not all the time but mostly when he sits or stands up."

"Well, that explains it," Steve said. "And after all, he is eleven years old now. We've been wondering why Charlie doesn't like to sit at the street corner before crossing anymore—you know, like he was trained to do."

"And," I said, "he's stopped jumping up on people, and doesn't run around and play like he used to. I just thought he'd outgrown that. Oh, I feel horrible. I should've known."

"Don't," Carol said. "Now you know. And you can get him some treatment. Chiropractic support may really help him."

"I'll check into that. So what about getting a second dog? Would Charlie mind? I don't have any immediate plans to get one, but just want to know how he'd react if I did. He's such a mamma's boy."

"He says he wouldn't mind as long as it's a male puppy or dog with a different purpose other than protection. He says he doesn't want a female dog. He says female dogs can sometimes be too uppity."

Steve stifled a laugh and reached down to give Charlie a ruffle on the head. Charlie picked his head up and looked at us like, "Huh?"

"Uppity?" I laughed too. "I guess guys are guys, no matter the species, right? My next question is about his protectiveness and dog aggression. *What* is that about?"

"He says he knows he's difficult. But he says that when he barks and carries on, he is carrying out his purpose. He says that as far as he is concerned, his purpose is to keep you safe no matter what. And he's quite proud of how he performs his role, thank you very much—and he intends to continue. He says that when he barks at another dog, he wants them to know that he is the boss and what he's saying to them is, 'STAY AWAY FROM MY MOM!'"

I was speechless. Again, there was no possible way Carol could have known that a week prior to this session, while taking Charlie for a walk, I "heard" or felt those *exact* words from him—even with the same inflection she gave—when he had barked at another dog. I kept this to myself. This had to be coincidence, right?

"Any questions from you, Steve?" Carol asked.

"No, I'm satisfied. I love him and he loves me back. I don't need to know anything else."

"Well, thank you, Carol!" I said. "This session has truly been an eye-opener!" We talked for a few more minutes and said goodbye.

"Wow!" I said, sitting back in my chair. "I need to absorb this."

Steve got up and grabbed Charlie's leash. "C'mon, Charlie. Your mom needs some time alone. Let's go find some uppity bitches to bark at!"

"Ve-ry funny!" I said, amused at Charlie's let's-hurry-up-and-go prance.

The house quiet, Charlie's words played in my head. "Think about it! Go within!" I thought about how many times I'd received that message lately. Had I listened? No. But receiving this message from Charlie made me sit up and take notice of what I'd been ignoring. I hadn't been giving enough attention to my *true* inner voice, my inner Self, my intuition. I suddenly realized this most integral, authentic part of my being was begging—*screaming*—to be accepted, acknowledged, and nurtured. In hearing these words from Charlie, I realized what had never occurred to me—that *he* would be one of my spiritual teachers.

~

To treat Charlie's hip discomfort, I scheduled weekly veterinary appointments for alternating chiropractic and acupuncture treatments. This increased his mobility quite a bit and a more playful Charlie resurfaced. While these treatments were an easy solution, my curiosity about animal communication was becoming a preoccupation with not-so-easy answers.

First of all, I wanted to know how to tell if you were making something up or actually receiving a telepathic message. As I reflected on my years with Charlie, I remembered several instances that could have been considered telepathic communication, but I wasn't sure.

I remembered the countless times when Charlie wasn't in the room with me and I would get a flash of awareness that he wanted a drink of water. I would inevitably find him patiently and silently waiting by the bathtub faucet (his preferred water source) with an appreciative look, saying, "Thanks for finding me. Could you turn this on, please?" Was this telepathy or simply my knowing his behavior pattern? Hmmm . . .

I also reflected on a time, years earlier, when I finally came to terms with my exasperation over Charlie's incessant barking at anything that had the audacity to so much as move in our front yard. Charlie considered himself not only my watchdog, but also the self-appointed watchdog for the entire neighborhood. He loved sitting at his post by the front window doing sentry duty. As soon as anything—bird, a neighbor pulling in or out of their *own* driveway, a cat, duck, person, dog or, God forbid, the dreaded enemy: the UPS truck (which he knew by sound before it came into sight)—entered "his" territory, he barked incessantly until the intruder was well out of sight. Nothing would quiet him. I would ask him to be quiet; I would attempt to reason with him. Sometimes, in total desperation, I would scream at him to shut up, which only left me feeling terrible and distant from him.

One day, when he was about five years old, he was ferociously barking at something he deemed not fit to be in his yard when he turned to me, and I *felt* him say, "Mom! Come here and look!" In that instant, I realized that in all those years of barking at passersby, that's all he had wanted me to do. When I knelt at the window beside him, he instantly forgot the trespasser and rewarded me with the sweetest, most exuberant kisses. I understood that the gratitude he expressed wasn't so much because I had joined him at the window, but that I'd finally "heard" him. I had *finally* understood him. All he had wanted was an alliance with me, to show me what was there, to give him reassurance that all was okay and acknowledgement that he was doing a good job as my protector. So was *that* experience telepathic communication?

What I did know was that when I joined him at the window that day, it was a turning point in our relationship. I shifted from merely thinking of him as my beloved dog, to yet a deeper perception of him as a beloved fellow being, a dog-being. The memory of this realization moves me to this day. From then on, whenever possible, I joined him at the window to scope out the trespasser and assure him all was well. Finally it dawned on me why this team effort comforted him. In his pack mentality, he was okay with being the watchdog, but he needed to know he had backup.

These instances, which seemed as though they could possibly be telepathic communication, made me yearn to know more about it. But what I really wanted to know was . . . could I do it?

Encounters of the Animal Kind

At Carol's introductory workshop I purchased the book *Animal Talk* by Penelope Smith, renowned pioneer in the field of animal communication and Carol's teacher. It had been lying around my house for several weeks, unread. So when, a few weeks later, my mother needed my help in taking care of her ten dogs, six cats, and twelve horses on her North Carolina farm while she recovered from surgery, I tossed Penelope's book into my suitcase. My weeks taking care of my mother's menagerie would be the perfect time to explore animal communication further.

My first experience was with my mother's golden retriever, Rocky. Rocky always ran away if given the chance and with no fenced-in yard, he had to be walked on a leash. Late one night while walking him, I was tired and wanted him to do his business so I could go to bed. Rocky had other things in mind. He urinated and began slowly meandering all over the yard. Because he wasn't allowed to run free, I indulged him his wanderings. Chilled by the frosty night air, I couldn't wait to crawl into my warm, cozy feather bed. Yet when I tugged on his leash, telling him we were going inside, I felt or "heard" him say, "But I have to poop!" At which point he took two small steps forward, squatted, and pooped. My mouth stood agape. It was as though I had never before witnessed such an occurrence. "Okay," I whispered up to the cloudy night sky, "is this your idea of some kind of crappy cosmic joke?" It *had* to be pure coincidence, my analytical mind told me. Yet I was intrigued by the way in which I had received the communication from Rocky. It wasn't like thinking a thought in my own mind, but rather like an instant knowing that almost intruded on my own thoughts, an intuitive type of feeling similar to those I'd had with Charlie.

I decided to experiment with animal communication to try to ease my lifelong fear of horses. I had not grown up with horses, and I had avoided them ever since my mom purchased the farm.

Now here I was, faced with the challenge of feeding and taking care of them—all twelve of them. Just the thought of getting them all in the barn and giving them their feed made me want to hyperventilate. But I had pushed my fear aside and walked down to the barn to say hello to them. As I approached, three horses waited for me at the barn gate. Before I got a chance to offer my greetings, a chestnut horse with a big, white blaze on its nose greeted me first. The horse made no physical movement, but I had the distinct sensation of being zapped with a powerful welcome. It was an enveloping, warm feeling that instantly melted my heart. I was greatly humbled. I, with my sense of human superiority, had thought I would bless them with my greeting. Yet it was she who greeted me. After being knocked off my high horse by a horse, my humility enabled my heart to open, and I explained my dilemma to the horses.

"Okay, guys," I said to my curious equine audience, "here's the deal. I have to take care of you for a while and I don't know how. I don't understand horses. You guys scare the heck out of me because you're so big and strong. But I want to understand you and not be afraid of you. So I'm leaving it up to you to teach me about horses."

My hoofed audience members snorted and twitched their ears as if listening attentively. I sensed that they were quite amused yet feeling affection towards me, and that these three willing partners would teach me what I yearned for as long as my heart remained open to them.

Day by day, my fear of them lessened. Yet feeding them was overwhelming, and my mom recruited a neighbor to help me. I understood from them that they didn't want me to fear them but rather to understand and appreciate them—not only as individuals, but as "horse." I felt that they could see deep inside me, to my core, and no matter who I was or wasn't, it was perfectly okay with them. Feeling this acceptance, I was able to trust and open my heart to them further. Their message seemed to be one of honesty—not only being honest with them, but with myself—to be more in touch with my feelings. If I was afraid, for instance, I needed to acknowledge it, accept it, and take action or get help so I could move on.

I had read that in legends, horses often bridge the realms of the spiritual and physical worlds. I could sense this otherworldly wisdom and essence in them. They seemed delighted at my attempt to communicate with and understand them. And I began to have a deep respect, bordering on awe, for their majestic spiritual nature. In those weeks on the farm I fell in love with horses and will be forever grateful for the lessons in authenticity they taught me.

But it was my mother's horse, Greta, who helped me to confirm that animal communication wasn't purely coincidental.

One lazy afternoon while I sat reading *Animal Talk*, my mother and I heard frantic whinnying from the pasture. I ran outside and saw Greta galloping from one corner of the pasture to an opposite corner where the rest of the herd was grazing peacefully. Physically, she seemed fine. However, the instant I saw her, my body tensed with panic and inside myself I heard, "I'm alone!" When she joined the other horses, all seemed well. So I went back inside.

"Was that Greta?" my mom asked.

"Yeah."

"Figures," my mom said. "She *hates* to be alone. She grazes and doesn't notice the other horses moving away and then freaks out when she finds herself alone."

"Oh . . . " was all I managed to say.

My analytical mind was beginning to accept that I was, indeed, communicating telepathically with animals. I felt I'd been given a precious key to the secrets of the universe. And the beauty of the key was in its simplicity—to be accepting, respecting, and loving of all forms of life—and in being so, my heart expanded to theirs and theirs to mine.

Now I *had* to learn more. I couldn't think of anything I wanted more than a deeper awareness of life and All That Is. And animals would be my teachers! I felt like a kid on Christmas morning who'd finally received the present she'd always wished for.

Toby

My perception of life had been changed because of awareness unleashed through animal communication. And now my life was about to change even more because of Toby, another black standard poodle.

My mom got Toby after Teddy, the poodle puppy she had taken from the same litter as Charlie, died tragically at only four months old. Teddy had been my mom's best buddy and when he died, she was heartbroken. Several months later, she got Toby from the same breeder's next litter (making Toby and Charlie half brothers). Sadly, Toby was never able to replace Teddy in my mother's heart.

When Toby was about five years old, he began to be a challenge for my mom. Jealous of the pampering received by a newly rescued golden retriever, Toby started urinating in the house. Given all her other dogs, cats, horses, and cows, my mom didn't have time to work with Toby to understand or correct his misbehavior. Instead, she sent him to the "slammer"—an outdoor kennel on her farm where he lived for several years with another behaviorally challenged dog. Toby was well fed, groomed, and given regular veterinary care, but received minimal affection. When I arrived at the farm that fall, his emotional fragility from the long-term lack of emotional and physical closeness was heartbreakingly palpable.

My sweet Toby boy

In my attempt to communicate with him, I understood that he felt he'd been "thrown away." I also understood that when my mother rescued the golden retriever, Toby felt rejected. Toby hadn't meant to misbehave or displease her—he simply knew no other way to express his discontent. His peeing in the house had been a cry for attention to regain her favor.

Thinking that I might be able to mend their relationship, I brought Toby in the house to live during my stay, as I'd done on previous visits. He behaved himself and did not urinate inside. I hoped my mom would see what a great, loving dog Toby was, and realize she had misunderstood him.

But a few days before my departure, out of the blue, she casually said, "Why don't you take Toby home with you?" My anger started to rise at her attempt to cast off Toby like an old pair of boots.

"Mom," I said, jaw clenched, "Toby is a nice dog."

"Well, I got Toby to replace Teddy," she replied matter of factly. "No dog could replace Teddy. Toby was a mistake."

Mistake? The word kicked me hard in the gut. And the shock of hearing it anesthetized my tongue. But my blood was starting to boil.

"Besides," Mom went on, "he's stupid. I can't get rid of him. Nobody wants him."

Rage seethed inside me like a rumbling volcano. I knew if I didn't leave immediately, blistering hot words would spew—words I would regret. I fled the house, taking Toby with me.

We retreated to a cabin on her property. Agitated, I began to clean the place like a whirling dervish. Just *what* was my mother's problem, I wondered as I angrily scrubbed the shower. She had rescued countless dogs and cats and done everything she could to return them to health. She had to be blind to not see Toby for the sweet and *smart* dog he was. Now that I knew her true feelings, I had to take him home with me.

But I worried about Charlie's reaction. Toby and Charlie had always gotten along well and were quite fond of each other. But would Charlie be okay with Toby living with us? Toby desperately needed and deserved a home where he was understood, appreciated, and loved, but my loyalty was to Charlie.

Surveying the now-sparkling cabin, my rage spent, I sat in a rocking chair to ponder. What, I wondered, had "pushed my buttons" to produce such an emotional tidal wave? Something had triggered it. Maybe it was time to clean my own "house" and clear out some old cobwebs.

Toby as a puppy, enticing Charlie to play

But first I needed to know if Charlie would accept Toby. That night I called Carol Schultz for a session. Through Carol, Charlie said he would, after adjusting, be fine with having Toby. And Toby, at his wit's end emotionally, said he would love to come home with me. Nevertheless, I was still extremely anxious about whether this was truly the right thing to do.

By the next afternoon I was frenzied about the situation. On the outside it looked simple: Toby wanted and needed a new home. Charlie was fine with it. Steve loved Toby and said he welcomed him. I wanted Toby. So what was my problem? What was this anxiety about?

I called my friend Lise, who worked with troubled employees and was accustomed to receiving frantic calls at work.

"Wow," Lise sighed after I explained the situation. "Your buttons really did get pushed! Do you think it

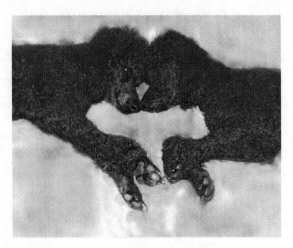

Charlie and Toby—the "Poodle Heart" photo

could be because *you've* felt misunderstood by your mom in the past—or unloved by your family?"

"Oh, ouch!" I winced. "Just hearing you say that brings it all up again. Yeah, I guess you hit the nail on the head."

"But here's the cool thing," Lise said.

"Yes, *please* tell me the cool thing," I said eagerly.

"In taking Toby, we know you're getting a sweet, smart, loving dog. But what you're also getting is the opportunity to heal the part of you that feels victimized and misunderstood—by anyone. Quite a gift from the Universe I'd say, huh girlfriend?"

"Yeah!" I said and paused. "You're right! You're absolutely right! I knew you'd figure it out for me! But . . . hey . . . wait . . . I don't like this," I said with uncertainty.

"What?!"

I sighed. "This means that now I have to take responsibility for my own healing, doesn't it? And I can't blame anybody else for what's happened to me . . . "

"Don't you hate being an adult sometimes?" Lise said wistfully.

"YEAH! But I don't have to start today, do I?"

"Nah!" she chuckled. "Give it a day or two!"

~

During the last days at my mom's farm I repeatedly told Toby that he was coming home with me. The morning we left, I packed the car and then opened the back door for Toby to get in. Instead of casually hopping in like he usually did, a black blur zoomed past me and landed on the seat, looking back at me with an expression that said, "Let's GO!"

As we drove down the wooded, gravel driveway of my mom's farm, I realized that the nurturing and love that I would give Toby for his healing would flow back to me for my own.

I began to see that my anger at my mother's inability to give me what I needed was only a mirror for what I hadn't been able to give myself. Didn't I often reject my own inner voice? Hadn't I often forgone self-compassion and self-love? My anger at my mother for not recognizing Toby for who he was and for not recognizing who *I* was had also been misdirected. Had *I* recognized myself? No. It was much easier to be a victim than to face the truth of who was really to blame. It hadn't been my mother—or anyone else for that matter—holding me back from standing in my own truth, power, and light. It was no one's fault but my own. And in time, I understood my mother's depth of grief over her beloved Teddy and forgave her harshness with Toby.

From this, several lessons became solidified in me. One: the Universe is indeed meant to heal us and is *never* out to cause us pain—even though it may sometimes seem that way. Two: everything truly does happen for a reason. Three: things are not always as they appear.

~

The first night that I arrived home with Toby, the two "brothers," not having seen each other in a year, postured and grumped. Steve and I took them for a walk and Toby, more interested in his surroundings than in looking where he was going, continually bumped into Charlie. Each bump extracted a quiet but warning growl from Charlie. But after this night of "bump and grump," they became inseparable, frequently sleeping curled up next to each other. Toby adored and looked up to his big brother (and never once urinated in the house). He totally accepted Charlie as the alpha dog. Charlie loved the canine camaraderie and never minded sharing me or his life with Toby—except for when Toby hogged the couch. For Steve and me, Toby was the piece of us we didn't know was missing until we discovered it. Toby, with his elegant demeanor and sweet, soft, unassuming personality, was a perfect fit.

In his new life, Toby blossomed. He became much more trusting, confident, and outgoing. Toby conveyed to Carol Schultz that in coming to live with us he felt like a puppy again, wanting to "see things and go places."

Gentle and shy, Toby was not at all a protective dog. He preferred to *be* protected. I remembered what Charlie

**Charlie (left) and Toby
enjoying a sunny winter day**

conveyed to me in that first session with Carol Schultz. Charlie had said that he wouldn't mind another dog in the family as long as it was a male dog with a purpose other than protection.

What, Exactly, Is Animal Communication?

U pon returning home from the farm, I read every book on animal communication I could get my hands on.

What I learned is that it is not a special gift reserved for the few—*everybody* has the ability to communicate telepathically with animals. Humans and animals are energy beings (meaning we—and they—are comprised of the energy of atoms and molecules), and communicate using various forms of non-verbal, or intuitive communication. We do this whether we're aware of it or not. The only advantage an animal communicator has is that he/she re-learns or remembers how to tune in and listen to (or feel) the non-verbal, intuitive communication being conveyed. Some may be more skilled than others, but anyone can do it. The biggest hurdle is ignoring the doubt that says you can't—or the voice that dismisses the information received.

The existence of telepathy is a stumbling block for many people. Indeed, there is no scientific proof that it occurs. Something so intangible and outside the confines of the mind is challenging to accept. Although I had read that scientists were beginning to see glimpses of connectedness in the Universe through the related activity of subatomic particles, the fact remains that there is no proof. For now, my intellect needed more sustenance regarding telepathy but what I longed for most was the only proof that would matter in my heart and mind—my own experience.

In *Animal Voices: Telepathic Communication in the Web of Life*, animal communicator Dawn Baumann Brunke says, "In the larger expanse of human history, communicating with animals is really nothing new. Our ancestors did it. Though, of course, the world was different then; humans had not yet forgotten. We were still connected to all—land and sky and water, wolf and buffalo, raven and sea turtle and spider and all other living things, which was everything because everything was alive. There was a single language. Do you remember? It was a language of being, where the smallest was joined to the largest, all things not apart, but a part of the All."

The books I read said that the energy we're made of is not limited to the physical body. However, even though scientists have confirmed that *all* living things—not only humans—have an essence, or field (also known as an "energy" field), that extends beyond the physical body, their research is mainly confined to the specifics of the material/physical world. They are not able to measure outside of it. These scientifically unsubstantiated, non-physical essences, according to my reading, are how indigenous cultures of ages past were able to communicate with nature and with each other over long distances. But in today's society, as Dawn Baumann Brunke's quote says, we have forgotten these essences that allow an exchange of information between another being—as in the case of an animal to a human and vice versa.

Most people have probably felt the presence of a person or animal approaching without seeing or hearing them. This sensing can result from them entering your essence field, which extends a few feet beyond the body. Whether or not you sense them depends on your level of awareness in that moment.

When someone experiences a "knowing" of something happening to a close friend or family member hundreds of miles away with no "proper" form of communication, this is known as a telepathic communication. A common definition of telepathy is "feeling at a distance"—a state of awareness finely tuned to the non-physical essence, or Spirit, of another being, either human or animal. Since telepathy is not bound by a structure of physical dimension, physical distance does not matter—you can be two feet away or a continent away and perceive information telepathically. It's sort of like a wireless connection.

Animals are innately in tune with physical energies and the non-physical Spirit essence of all beings. This explains the "phenomenon" of animals getting excited about their person's homecoming when the person is still ten minutes from home, or how an animal knows you're going on a trip before you start to pack your suitcase, or how Charlie magically knew when I needed comforting. Animals are masterful at picking up on our thoughts, emotions, and physical energy (and also Earth energies, as has been demonstrated with tsunamis and other weather catastrophes—or "weather vane" dogs who sense a storm coming long before it's on the radar). Although most domesticated animals have the ability to understand spoken words, this reading of non-physical essence is their true "language."

In other words, an animal can understand our thoughts regardless of whether they are in words or images. This is demonstrated frequently in horseback riding. Trainers tell riders to simply form an image in their minds of what they want the horse to do.

I learned that another example is in teaching a dog not to bark. Oftentimes, the command "No bark!" is given. But while saying these words, it's nearly impossible *not* to have the image of the barking dog in your head. While the dog may understand the word "no," he also gets the barking image being sent to him. This can be confusing. Our words and mental images should be congruent. So in this case, asking the dog to "Be quiet!" or "Shhh!" can be more effective. I sure wish I had known this when Charlie was younger!

So what an animal communicator does is tune into the essence, or Spirit, of an animal via a meditative state to perceive information. Some animal communicators prefer to have a photo. Once perceptions are received through the communicator's "filtering system," then the perception is formed into words. This is similar to a foreign language translator paraphrasing something. An animal communicator gets the gist of the animal's truth that is being conveyed. Ultimately, it depends on how the information is interpreted. Though trained to listen keenly, with purity of intuitive heart, an animal communicator's capacity to accurately interpret the information is only as good as his or her ability to perceive and translate it.

One key element that separates animals from humans is intellect. Animals rely mostly on instinct and do not use mental analysis in the way that humans do. Lacking this, it can be said that animals don't question or doubt their spiritual connection as humans do and are able to maintain their constant connection to who they are as spiritual beings.

And so we find ourselves with a great paradox. On the one hand, man possesses his unique form of intellect, making him the only being capable of seeking and understanding his Source, or God. This seeking of God, I believe, is the purpose of life. Yet animals, while lacking this intellect, don't lose their awareness as spiritual beings, and thus, provide us with unconditional love. It seems God, in his infinite compassion, gave us animals to help us find our way back to Him.

After learning all of this, I was still puzzled by one thing. If animals lack our intellect, then how can animal communicators perceive words or thoughts of wisdom from them? When I looked at Charlie in his standard poodle body, I was baffled at how he could be capable of telling me to "go within." But I began to understand that information received by animal communicators comes from the animal's spiritual Self—their Spirit essence, the non-physical consciousness that we all possess and share.

This idea of animals possessing a spiritual Self wasn't new to me and I had already begun to view Charlie as an equal fellow being. But slowly now, I was beginning to have a deeper appreciation for all life. What is life on this planet, I mused, if not a gigantic ecosystem dependent on *all* beings? I had once heard it said that if humans were wiped off the face of the Earth, the Earth could survive. However, if ants were eradicated, the Earth couldn't sustain itself very long. Man may be the King of Creation, but who deemed him superior?

I began to dream of a world where *all* animals are treated with the recognition that they, too, are spiritual beings. And where every being—with legs, wings, or fins—is treated with just as much respect as humans.

After reading of various authors' profound experiences with animal communication, I found myself yearning even more for similar experiences of my own. And I longed for deeper insight into Charlie and Toby—to be able to speak *their* language and grow spiritually with and because of them. Even more than that, I felt an underlying desperation to know that I would be able to communicate with them after they died. Then they would never be "gone."

Now what I needed was to further my life experience and gain competency at my intuitive communication skills. I was itching to take a class.

Wings to Soar

The following spring I took a two-day basic workshop on animal communication with Carol Schultz in the Chicago area.

The key to learning animal communication, or any intuitive process, Carol explained, is to learn to thoroughly listen within. Because everyone perceives intuitions differently—there is no right or wrong way—it's important to learn which unique "modus operandi" each individual perceives with—images, intuitive-knowings, physical sensations, direct thoughts, or any combination or all of these.

In order to do this, the key is to listen not with the mind but with an expanded awareness. In the meditative exercises, this, for me, felt like listening through my heart. When I closed my eyes, I felt my being soften and expand, like it did when gazing out at a breathtaking landscape—with little awareness of body or mind—just taking in the wonder.

We practiced communicating with animals that Carol had brought photos of, learning how we perceive and discerning the difference between our own mind and telepathy.

I had to keep relaxing with expanded awareness, continually letting go of mental chatter to listen, feel, and allow perceptions to come. It was similar to walking in nature while lost in thought—birds are singing but you don't hear them because you're thinking about what is on your "to-do" list. Then you're aware of a bird landing on a tree branch nearby, which awakens you to the chorus of birdsong surrounding you. It's delightful, so you begin to listen, and with expanded awareness, you start to distinguish the song of a cardinal from that of a goldfinch. Tuning in even more closely, you can begin to discern the song of an individual cardinal.

Mostly, my perceptions came via intuitive-knowings—which are feelings that come in a flash and require no thought, as if the information is just "there." Yet oftentimes it was too vague and very hard to interpret. And although Carol told us over and over not to discount *any* perceptions, no matter how they came, I had choruses of doubting voices. She assured us that in time, if we strengthened our intuitive muscle, mostly by speaking our perceptions and getting confirmation, these doubting voices would become whispers. I couldn't wait for that day to come.

The first night, at home, I practiced my homework assignment, which was to ask our own animals what message they had for us regarding the class.

Snuggling with Charlie on the couch, I took a few breaths, quieted myself, and melted into his essence. Mentally I asked him, "What do you want to tell me about this class?"

His response zinged back at me, faster than I could form a thought. "You can do it. Just trust yourself!" Charlie . . . my consummate source of support.

Of Toby, I asked if he would like to come with me the next day, since on the last day of class we were asked to bring our animals. For obvious reasons, taking Charlie to a room with other dogs was out of the question. With Toby, trying out a different technique, I spoke aloud, pausing to adequately visualize each phrase. "We'll go for a long ride in the car. Then we'll sit in a room with other dogs, maybe some cats or birds. You'll have to sit still and be quiet. The people will welcome you and be friendly. It will be a long day. I would love for you to come with me." I paused and then added, "But I'm not sure you'll like it."

His response came, again as an intuitive-knowing, with a hint of amusement. "Mom, you worry too much! I'll be fine." And he was. He proved to be a perfectly behaved gentleman in a room full of other dogs, cats, birds, turtles, and fish. At one point when he'd had enough with the fidgety, whining dog behind him, he turned and delivered a low, non-menacing "Knock it off!" growl. The dog quieted.

During the class I realized that another divine gift had been given to me when Toby came to live with us. I understood that Charlie accepted he couldn't do certain things with me, and that part of Toby's role was to be Charlie's emissary. The pride that Toby exhibited during the class that day made me understand that he reveled in this responsibility.

With the array of species available to communicate with in the workshop, we learned that all animals communicate in the same manner. Communicating with a cat, for example, is the same as with a turtle; each simply experiences life differently.

An African gray parrot was my most valuable teacher. We did an exercise where we chose an animal in the room to communicate with. We were told not to ask any specific question, but to remain open for a few minutes and just allow information to come. Sitting across the room from the parrot, I focused my attention on him, expanded my awareness, and melted into his essence. I suddenly felt as if I were in a smoke-filled room. I felt a smoky haze and faintly smelled cigarette smoke—though there was none in the room. I also felt a vague but distinguishable respiratory heaviness. I understood via an intuitive-knowing that he wanted his human to stop smoking because it was bothering him and it was also bad for her. He wanted her to know that he supported her desire to quit. Not knowing *anything* about this person (there were twenty people in the class and I didn't even know whose parrot it was), I was extremely reluctant to share this information. I doubted myself and feared looking foolish if I was wrong. But I was keen to know if I'd perceived correctly, so I shared the information with the class. It turned out that the parrot's person did smoke, and that she was struggling with quitting.

Observing the parrot in his cage, I had also asked him if he missed being able to fly and be free. He said not really because he was happy with his life but also that he had learned to "fly and soar from within." While perceiving this from him, I received a feeling of such ecstatic freedom and joy that I actually felt I was soaring. I wondered if this ecstasy was similar to what the ancient mystics referred to when recounting their meditation experiences of "going within to other realms." Whether it was or not, this brief incident of utter bliss left me wanting more.

After the workshop, I began to claim my intuition, which allowed me to be more open and available to Charlie and Toby. I didn't get as exasperated with Charlie when he spun into his protective frenzies. By staying grounded, I helped him regain his composure and slightly lessened his need to be so protective.

"You know," Steve said, "I'm starting to notice that Charlie is more confident because you're more confident. And I think he's relieved that you understand him better. It's a mutual stress reducer."

With Toby, I recognized that what I had misinterpreted as shyness was really a soothing and delightful gentleness. This recognition changed how both Steve and I interacted with him. We stopped trying to make him socialize. "He's just happy being Toby," Steve said. And as we allowed Toby to be just who he was, he began to blossom.

"Have you noticed Toby's new stride?" Steve asked. "It's more like a prance—like he's happy and proud to be himself."

These insights brought a deeper level of comfort and understanding to my relationships with the boys. In fact, this applied to *all* my boys—Steve included.

"Sometimes I hesitate to share my insights or experiences with you," I told Steve one day. "I'm afraid you'll think I'm nuts."

"Well, only for a second or two," he laughed. "No, really, I don't think you're nuts. They're your experiences. I can't always relate, but I find it fascinating. I like hearing about it."

"Does what I share help you relate more to the boys?" I asked.

"Yeah," he thought for a moment. "It does. I don't see them as just pets anymore. Now they're more like good friends. Now I know animals are just like us emotionally. I never knew that before."

I found that Steve's increased closeness with the boys, in turn, made me appreciate them more, too. And, of course, witnessing his increased tenderness towards

Charlie and Toby made my heart swell with appreciation for Steve, and we grew closer as a result.

"You know," Steve said, "we're not a couple with two dogs anymore. We're really a family."

I couldn't have agreed more.

Although the basic workshop had given me some confidence in my intuitive communication abilities, I knew that I still had a long way to go to become proficient. I became obsessed with improving my intuitive skills and experiencing more inner truths.

∿

Four months later, with Steve's encouragement to "stay the course!" I left my boys at home and took off for Point Reyes, California, to take two advanced classes over ten days from the renowned animal communicator, Penelope Smith.

Sitting in my room the night before the first class began, I was wracked with fear and doubt. My mind screamed at me, *What on Earth possessed you to spend all this money to fly across the country and study this weird stuff? What have you gotten yourself into?* I had almost convinced myself that any telepathic validation I'd received at my mom's farm or in Carol's class was a fluke. I wanted to run away.

Then I reminded myself of the deeper connection I wanted to feel with Charlie and Toby and my yearning to be able to communicate with them even after they died. And still I wanted to turn tail and run.

Desperate, I called Steve.

"I'm freaking out! I need a pep talk."

"I thought this was what you wanted to do," he said, surprised.

"It is. I mean . . . I thought it was. Damn! I don't know!"

"Well," he said calmly after listening to my litany of anxieties, "just do it for Charlie." Charlie. Instantly, I felt my courage and resolve returning. "I know you're doing this for all of us—Charlie, yourself, Toby, and me." It was so like Steve to put himself last. "So when you're unsure of why you're there, just think of Charlie."

Steve's rationale helped me put things in perspective. And then I was able to remind myself of my life philosophy—to avoid regrets whenever possible. My even greater fear, I realized, was that if I didn't stick this out, I could lose out on something big, maybe even bigger than I could imagine. This cinched my decision to stay—that, and the fact that it was late at night and the San Francisco airport was a two-hour drive away.

Sipping my tea in the little garden the next morning, I listened to the birds warble a cheery welcome to the new day. It seemed they were singing of promise, which was refreshing after a fitful night's sleep. With the perspective of a fresh, new day, I understood that the previous night's doubts and misgivings were none other than sheer terror. Coming to this course, I realized, was a monumental moment of truth. Somewhere, my subconscious recognized that my life was about to change profoundly. Once I walked through the door, there would be no turning back.

An hour later I drove up the twisting, mountainous road through lush, wooded landscape to Penelope's house. As I ascended, I left the morning fog behind. But could I leave behind my fog of fear? As I drove slowly, I was mesmerized by the way the sunshine danced its way through the branches of the majestic redwoods and pines. Everything seemed *alive*. Or maybe it was just my angst that heightened my sensitivities. I rolled my window down a bit and the crisp, cool, woodsy-smelling air rushed in. It was both exhilarating and calming. A hawk soared above and I felt as though I was entering the *Twilight Zone*—that these were all props of an enchanted stage being set for me. Just *what*, I wondered with an odd mixture of trepidation and excitement, would the next week and a half bring to my life?

I parked the car and walked through the gate of Penelope's house, but then didn't have a clue where to go from there. Just when an apprehensive voice in my head said, *This is it! Your last chance to bolt!* I saw an adorable orange cat—his gaze fixed on me—slowly approaching from the garden.

He came within ten feet, looking at me as though he had the answer to everything, then turned and began walking back through the garden. Feeling somehow under his spell, I followed him. He led me through a garden of roses and colorful wildflowers, and around the house to the back door where, through large picture windows, I could see other people milling around.

He stopped at the door, glanced up as if to say, "Enter here," and with his mission accomplished, sauntered off into the bushes. This would not be the only time that Penelope's little orange magician, named Sherman, would leave his paw print on my heart.

Penelope greeted me with a hug. "There you are!" she said. Her warmth relaxed me a bit and I began to think I would survive after all.

∾

The other thirteen students and I sat in a semicircle in Penelope's living room. The comforting peachy wall color, animal print cushions, and wood-burning stove felt homey, and I started to relax. Her dogs and cats wandered in and out, sometimes choosing a lap to cuddle in.

I expected Penelope's classes to be somewhat the same as Carol's basic class. They were, only a *lot* more challenging. Any bit of cockiness I walked in with quickly disappeared. What was totally unexpected was the deep introspection that occurred during our work. Because animal communication sessions can often range in time from ten minutes to over an hour, being able to stay present in an expanded state of awareness is essential. The discipline of learning to quiet the mind and really listen *within*—instead of listening to mind chatter or outside distractions—was really tough.

During meditation exercises, my mind could stay peacefully quiet for about five minutes and then start chattering away with, *Wonder if I'm doing this right . . . Oh man, this exercise is taking forever. My back hurts. Boy, would I love a cup of Earl Grey tea with a splash of honey and milk. I miss Steve and the boys. Wonder what they're doing . . . What if I can't do this? What if I'm the only one in the class who doesn't get it?*

Intellectually I knew not to buy into the doubts. But now, the more I tried *not* to listen to my mind, the more it became like a petulant child demanding my attention: *You're not getting it! You're no good at this!* My mind told me this so often, I started to believe it.

"I don't know if I can do this," I told Penelope one morning before class.

"But you're not really *listening*," she said. "You're listening to your mind. Don't listen to your mind. Listen with telepathic 'ears.'"

"But I don't think I'm doing it right," I said in exasperation.

"You're a very high-strung person, Mary Ann," she said matter of factly. "You're rarely grounded because your mind is always spinning out."

I stared blankly at her, stunned by her candor. She continued, "But you're certainly not the only one and that's one reason why you're here—to learn a new way of being."

"Okay," I said, still reeling.

"It's all a part of the process."

"Okay," I said, suddenly wishing I wasn't a part of this blasted process.

"You'll be fine." She walked away, leaving me standing there feeling naked and defenseless. I crossed my arms and pulled them in, giving myself a hug. I would need to lick my wounds and mull this over.

Her critical words echoed in my head all day. Every once in a while I'd think, "God! What a bitch!" Other times I wanted to be rocked and comforted like a child.

At dinner that night a classmate I'd befriended, Kathleen, and I shared our highs and lows of the day.

"Well, here's my low," I said, recounting my conversation with Penelope.

"Ouch! She said that?" Kathleen said, stifling a laugh.

"Well, thanks for your compassion," I said, slapping a hunk of butter on a piece of cornbread.

"Well, Missy, I've only known you for three days, but I gotta tell 'ya, you are pretty hard on yourself. Do *you* think you're high-strung?"

"Well . . . yeah. My mind's been chewing on it all day," I said pushing a tomato around my plate. "Penelope's right. People have told me my whole adult life to 'mellow out,' but I could never understand what they were talking about. Now I get it. It's no wonder I've been struggling."

"So, tell me," Kathleen said. "Is your inner critic ruthless and relentless?"

"Yep. Pret-ty darn ruthless and relentless, all right."

"And are you a perfectionist who carefully crosses every 't' and then double checks just to make sure you did it right—and maybe checks even a third time just for good measure?"

I laughed. "So how long have you known me?"

"Yeah, well, I guess it takes one to know one," she said, and took a sip of tea.

"So," I asked, "are you also the proverbial 'what-if' person who worries about *everything*, like me?"

"No," she said with a playful glint in her eye, "I just expect everybody to do things my way. Then I don't have to worry!"

We cackled with laughter.

"So here's to us," I said, holding up my water glass. "Here's to learning a kinder way of being with ourselves."

"Hallelujah!" she cheered. "Here's to new beginnings!"

～

The next morning I wondered if I really could learn a new way of being more mellow and grounded. I had been so driven all my life. Now that I had acknowledged this high-strung aspect of myself, I didn't quite know what to do about it or how to change. I felt so cracked open, vulnerable, and confused. And I was embarrassed that I had been so blind to it for so long.

So with trepidation, I went to Penelope.

She said, "Don't blame yourself or feel ashamed. The changes aren't going to happen overnight. This is just the first step. You've got to hold yourself in compassion."

Hold myself in compassion? I never knew that was an option! And she made it sound so easy.

"Don't worry," she chuckled, seeing the helpless look on my face. "The animals are masters of compassion. They'll teach you. Start with giving yourself permission to cut yourself some slack."

I laughed. "You mean I'm allowed to do that?"

"It's a part of your awakening. We've all been through it," she said softly. "It's not always easy, but you're doing fine."

"Thanks," I said, sighing with relief.

Later that day I had another revelation—I realized that instead of the rigid, hard-nosed judge being in control of me, I could be in control of it. With this insight I was able to be a more open channel, and remain in a meditative state for a longer period of time. And even when my mind discounted my perceptions, I could accept it as part of the experience and choose not to listen to it.

Sherman, the little orange cat, again helped me find my way. As he lazed in the sun next to me on the deck after lunch one day, I said out loud, "Tell me, Master Sherman, how can I deepen my intuitive skills? How do I quiet my mind? What can I—" But before I could finish this last question, Sherman rolled over and looked at me with such intensity that I abruptly sat back in silence.

He continued to stare at me until I felt him impatiently say, "Listen! Just listen *inside!* That's *all* you have to do!"

"Got it," I said sheepishly. "Shut up and listen."

While doing the exercises over the next couple of days, I was better able to melt into a quiet place inside to "just listen." I was able to turn the volume down on the mental chatter and tune in to what I was recognizing as my intuitive channel. My confidence increased exponentially.

And then I failed—miserably. In one exercise, while communicating with a fellow participant's cat, Simba, my mind was frantically grabbing, reaching for information. I don't know if I was trying to prove my capabilities to myself or the class, but in any case, I didn't perceive anything accurately. Instead of opening myself to intuitive communication, my mind was manufacturing the answers. In front of the class, the cat's person repeatedly corrected me, "Well, no, actually, Simba *doesn't* like to go outside," and "No, she *is* declawed." And on it went.

"Well, that was painful," I said to Penelope at break.

"Yeah," she grimaced. "It was."

However, this "failure" proved to be a most ingenious teacher. It embedded in me the key principle of intuitive communication—the necessity for the mind to be a quiet and open channel to *allow* perceptions to come.

Paradoxically, it was the one image that Simba had relayed to me, which I had rejected, that proved to be correct. It faintly resembled an anatomy book photograph of Simba's kidneys. I could feel the energy in her kidneys was weak—sort of like a waning battery. But this perception had been almost imperceptible and because I hadn't gotten anything else right, I was afraid to mention it. However, during the break, Simba's person said the vet had recently told her that Simba's blood tests showed she had the beginning stages of kidney failure.

Here was the reality of telepathy—that it is usually so subtle it is ignored, overlooked, or denied.

≈

And so my failure turned into a valuable gift, teaching me how to discern telepathy from what my mind was creating. When I employed my mind on a seeking mission, it could come up with any number of answers or explanations—sort of like a guessing game. But when I chose to quiet my mind and allow awareness to expand, perceptions came in a dreamlike flash that, for lack of any better definition, felt like the intuitive-knowing of undeniable Truth—a certainty that was perceived faster than any thought could form in my mind.

This discernment of mind versus intuitive communication was put to the test on the last day. Instead of communicating with an animal, we were asked to go outside and communicate with something in nature—a tree, flower, butterfly, frog—whatever we felt drawn to.

"Or," Penelope said, pointing out the window, "you could communicate with one of those mountains." I giggled to myself. Animals were one thing, but communicate with a mountain? C'mon! She had to be joking. The serious look on her face revealed that she was not.

"Remember," Penelope said, "all things are connected. All things have an essence of Spirit; all things are part of Consciousness."

I wandered around the garden looking for some cute little critter to converse with. But my attention was drawn to the mountains across the valley. They were densely dotted with pines, as if they had gigantic green blankets draped over them. Captivated, I sat down Indian style on the spongy grass and noticed a patch of fog hiding the peak of the closest mountain. Even partially hidden, it was enormous and I felt intimidated by its magnitude. How could I communicate with it? I felt silly even trying. But right then, as if it heard my thoughts, the fog glided away and the mountain, in all its grandeur, was revealed. It was as if it were playfully saying, "Here I am. Come!"

I took a few deep breaths. *Just melt into it*, I told myself. I closed my eyes and relaxed. I felt my heart expand until it merged with the mountain. Tears tingled in my eyes as I felt an immense, loving presence, and it felt as though I was being cradled in the arms of a thousand loving, compassionate grandmothers.

"This is the love of the Earth!" I felt the mountain say. "It will always cradle you. Feel it! Feel it under your feet! It will support you. Honor you." I lingered in the bliss of this message, understanding that the Earth—the very "thing" I live on, walk on, and eat from, is a dear, dear ally.

With this experience, I was able to put to rest the occasional doubt that any of this was manufactured in my mind. The deep connection with the mountain had been so surprising, spontaneous, and moving. I had felt absolutely At One—such deep peace and acceptance. My mind had *never* before conjured up something as profound as this. Nor did I believe it capable of such profundity purely on its own.

I left the course feeling a whole new world had been opened up to me. Prior to this, I had simply been living life on Earth. Now, I felt privileged to live as a part of the Earth with all her beings. And in feeling this One with

All, I felt a deeper connection with myself and in turn, with the Divine. I didn't know how my day-to-day life with Charlie and Toby would be changed, but I was eager to find out.

~

Before leaving, I had my classmate, Kathleen, tune in to Charlie. Since he was turning twelve, I needed reassurance that he was okay physically.

"He says he's fine," she said. "He said he feels good, is really enjoying his life, but says not to worry." Then she laughed. "He says you worry too much about him."

"Who, me?"

Kathleen rolled her eyes.

~

In my heart, I also carried Penelope's code of ethics for animal communicators. This states the profession's intent to give compassionate, nonjudgmental care. It further states that ethically, an animal communicator can only do a reading if the animal's person has requested it, and that an animal communicator does not diagnose or treat illnesses.

~

The classes also gave me the awareness of how the spoken word—the very thing that separates man from animal—can be a hindrance. Because we humans use speech as our primary way of communicating, we are more focused externally than internally, and in doing so, we've gotten out of touch with our innate intuition.

But does our ability to form thoughts into language make us superior to other beings?

I learned that animals are easier to communicate with because they don't hide or deny their feelings or emotions like we do. Without the spoken word, animals—and even insects and plants—have much to tell and teach us. But we rarely acknowledge, much less use, our natural intuitive abilities to tune in to them. Why? Because our culture has conditioned us to believe that language is the only form of communication. Clearly, language has significance. What we've forgotten is the power in the subtle, silent language of intuitive awareness, known as telepathy.

To further emphasize this, Wyatt Webb, in his book *It's Not About the Horse: It's about Overcoming Fear and Self-Doubt*, states, "We're often led to believe that we connect through words, but it's been my experience that we actually use words more often to avoid communicating with each other." Language can keep us emotionally distant. It's easy to distance ourselves by veiling our feelings in words.

Also, words are often interpreted incorrectly, causing misunderstandings and unnecessary judgments. And lastly, language gives us the ability to tell lies—not only to each other, but to ourselves. Language may be a blessing, but in learning about intuitive awareness, we need to acknowledge that language is a double-edged sword.

≈

I was happy to be home with all three of my boys again. As strange as it may sound, I hadn't communicated tele-pathically with either Charlie or Toby while away. During the courses I needed to filter out my daily life, hunker down, and envelop myself in learning. But I had checked in with Steve each night, so I heard about Charlie and Toby's daily events of car rides and trips to the park, or their favorite special treat of Arby's roast beef. And most nights, Steve put the receiver to their ears so they could hear my voice.

Within days of returning home, I noticed that I was much more in sync with Charlie and Toby—there was more of an "us" rather than a "me-them" relationship. I felt deeper gratitude for having these beings in my life. I knew my poodles had oodles to teach me and I couldn't wait to know what spiritual lessons they had for me. So one afternoon I grabbed a pen and notepad with a journalist-style intention of asking them some questions. I was sitting next to Charlie on the floor, poised to quiet myself, when he looked up at me as if to ask, "What are you doing?"

I put the pen and notepad down and looked into his quizzical eyes. What was I doing? In my usual, driven way, I was set to sit down and get the facts—get to it and get it done. Wasn't this the part of me I wanted to change? Granted, I was a novice and I wanted to try things out by communicating with my own animals. But as I sat, gently massaging Charlie's shoulders, I realized the only thing I needed to do was simply be with them, stay connected with their essences. I knew that if I did this, their spiri-tual teachings would unfold. I needed to be patient—not easy for me. What I only realized later was that this was actually their first teaching—in order to stay connected to them I needed to remain grounded within myself.

Still, in a hidden corner of my mind was the concern about the numerous accounts I had heard regarding the difficulty of communicating with one's own animals. Our emotional attachments to them can be a hindrance to obtaining a clear message. And, with Charlie almost twelve years old, even though he had told Kathleen he was physically fine, I fretted about his aging and physical health. I feared I couldn't "park" my emotions long enough to hear what he might have to say. Indeed, I needed to take things slowly and first learn to be with them.

After learning that animals oftentimes mirror their people by exhibiting behaviors the people do not see in themselves, I wondered what Charlie and Toby were mirroring. I came to recognize that Charlie's dog-aggressive protective frenzies mirrored my high-strung mental/emotional anxieties, the result of living in an ungrounded manner. This mirror wasn't an easy one to look into, but it reflected aspects of myself I knew desperately needed to be transformed. Toby, on the other hand, was my wise, gentle, laid-back mirror. Somewhere inside me was Toby's laid-back gentleness. If only I could see and find it.

The more I opened myself up to receive what Charlie and Toby had to teach me about myself, the more I felt equipped to give back to them—to understand what they needed. Also, believing I'd be able to connect with them after they died brought me some peace.

Steve's mind was eased, too. "I feel better knowing you can help interpret what these boys need," he said on an evening walk with them. "I want to give them the best and I don't like guessing what's going on with them."

Charlie studying the cover of Sonya Fitzpatrick's *What the Animals Tell Me*

"Oh yeah?" I said. "You always seem to know when they want Arby's!"

"Well, the only thing they've ever told me was that they wished Arby's was open 24/7!"

After Penelope's courses I knew I needed to practice, practice, practice. I did readings for my friends who were open to animal communication. These readings had reciprocal benefits—my friends said the readings gave them a deeper understanding and closer connection with their animals, and I gained confidence in my ability. But most importantly, being in a meditative state, I benefited from the experience of profound compassion while connecting with the spiritual essence of the animals. This infusion of compassion filled me with greater faith in the Divine.

Nevertheless, as much as I loved doing the readings, I was unsure about taking another step and doing animal communication professionally. I felt insecure about doing something considered strange by mainstream "society"—not to mention my family and a few friends. Although some of my family and friends accepted my seventeen-year path of Eastern philosophy and vegetarianism, for others, it was too much of a departure from their reality, and their comments sometimes carried underlying tones of sarcasm or ridicule. Was I going to tell them I was communicating with animals? Nope. No way. I was still too vulnerable and feared that their criticism might steer me away from this new and treasured part of my life. I'd tell them when I was ready.

One day I discussed my nervousness about accepting myself as an animal communicator with my friend Eve, who, as a Reiki Master and shamanic practitioner, understood the risk of ridicule by mainstream society. "Well, I understand your concerns," she said, shrugging nonchalantly. "But you need to just put yourself out there."

Just put myself out there? Risk being labeled a weirdo? I had expected Eve to coddle me a bit—not shove me face-first into reality.

"Why don't you get business cards made up?" she said, looking straight at me.

"Business cards?" I echoed. "But I'm not sure I want to do this professionally. Besides," I said, throwing up my hands in exasperation, "I still need time to practice."

But wise woman Eve knew that I was afraid.

"Get some business cards made," she repeated firmly. "Then you'll take yourself more seriously."

Oh, she just doesn't get it! I told myself. But I knew she was right and cursed the fact that I didn't have the guts to follow through with it. But a short while later, I did. It's funny to think that some little cards could make such a difference. Eve was right. Seeing the words

"Animal Communicator" under my name on those cards made me stand a little taller. I was proud of what I had accomplished—regardless of what anyone else thought. I tested the Universe by telling it that if I was meant to be a professional animal communicator, I needed a sign—a referral. Less than a week later, I got my first call. The woman on the phone said she had gotten my name from a friend, and was in desperate need of help with her three Rottweilers.

My shingle was hung.

My Animal Teachers

My heart sang with wanton glee now that I was more fully open to an intuitive way of communicating with all beings. However, my ego considered itself spiritually arrived, much in the same way a college graduate feels arrogantly competent to tackle the world. From my animal clients, I quickly discovered that compared to the spiritual wisdom of animals, I was a mere spiritual preschooler.

As I increasingly saw the world through animals' perspectives, I became amused at man's (and my own) odd behavior of invading their space with coos, pats, kisses, tweaks or hugs, without any regard for whether this is welcome. Imagine someone you don't know approaching you and, without your consent, putting their hands all over your face and/or body while talking gibberish! This may sound silly and I know that many times animals seek this attention and bask in it, but the point is that we do this based on our need without considering the animal's wants or needs. For me it was a paradigm shift to think of meeting an animal with the same respect as I would with another fellow human. I learned, when meeting an animal for the first time, to simply say hello and then allow them the space to dictate whether or not they welcomed further attention or affection. I noticed this helped build their trust.

Often, when I was walking Charlie or Toby in the neighborhood or park, children would run up to us, wanting to pet them. Fortunately, both Charlie and Toby loved children and welcomed this (it was only other dogs that induced Charlie's protectiveness). Nevertheless, when children ran up to us, I asked them to please walk, and asked them how they would feel if strangers suddenly ran up and surrounded them. I thought about my own childhood and wished I had been made aware of animals as sentient, fellow beings.

One lesson about respect towards animals came from Penelope's delightfully dignified Afghan hound, Buddha Boy. After lunch one day, I was leisurely walking around Penelope's property and saw Buddha Boy trotting my way. At first I thought he was coming to say hello but then noticed that his attention was focused on the happenings at the front gate. Missing Charlie and Toby and yearning for canine companionship, I called to him. He trotted over with an "I'm-kinda-busy-but-whatcha-got?" demeanor— no doubt hoping I'd saved him a morsel from lunch.

"I just wanted to say hi," I said, reaching out and tenderly rubbing his long, stately face. I could feel he was tolerating me and growing impatient. Then I gently brushed the tip of his nose with the knuckle of my index finger— an affectionate gesture I habitually did with Charlie and Toby.

Buddha Boy's eyes flashed with insult. He said "Don't treat me like a dog!" and trotted off in dignified disgust.

This lesson taught me that just because he was a dog didn't mean that I could treat him the same way I treated my own dogs. This insight was a welcome gift to my deeper awareness that every animal is a unique individual that deserves to be treated as such.

This lesson, however, was much more palatable than the one I received after offending Penelope's alpha llama, Regalo. Take it from me—it's not very wise to impose your authority over the alpha llama and insist on giving your banana peel to the less dominant, shy llama. Unless, of course, you're wearing protective spit gear!

Spiritually, I learned that just as with humans, some animals are more evolved than others—some are especially wise beings. Yet, all the same, all animals are spiritual beings.

Some animals are in their people's lives simply to have fun and love them unconditionally, with no "deeper" spiritual teaching. But what greater learning exists besides unconditional love?

I came to see that, commonly, animals mirror, or "shadow," aspects of their people—the aspects of ourselves that we find difficult to see, but once acknowledged, provide us with a chance to heal and grow. The best example of this was with a dog named Moxy. Moxy had many physical ailments and her person wanted to know why. Moxy said, "My mom needs things to take care of, so I give her things to take care of." When I relayed this to Moxy's person, she said, "Well, I am in counseling for co-dependency."

I believe the reason certain animals come in to our lives—and what they give and teach us—is orchestrated with Divine perfection. One of my favorite teachings—favorite because it was so simple, yet profound—was from Linus the cat. His person wanted advice on how to accept the shortcomings of other people. Feeling a seraphic calm emanating from him, Linus said, "Compassion. Compassion is the biggest Truth of all."

In communicating with animals near and after death, I learned that they do not fear it. Just like us, they do not want pain or suffering, but they do not fear death itself.

One memorable example was a session with a dying cat. The cat's person wanted to know her cat's perspective on its impending death. Matter of factly, the cat said that death was similar to changing jobs—that while she was here, she had served a purpose; when her body died, she would serve a purpose in Spirit form; and on the cycle went. Her essence never changed—only her experiences did.

And often our animals come back to us in the same animal form, or in a different one. While some animals prefer returning as the same species, a horse, for example, might return to the same person as a dog—if a dog is more suitable for the person's life at that time. However, the essence of Spirit remains the same, and therefore personality traits are recognizable when an animal returns in another body. For example, a cat that returns in another cat body might again display the unique behavior of leaving her toys in her food bowl. Or a horse that returns as a dog might run with a horse-like gait or nudge you in exactly the same way. Animals are truly angels, bringing us love, compassion, and many lessons.

Communicating with non-domesticated species is also enlightening. I came to understand that every species has a purpose and maintains a distinct energy to assist in balancing the Earth—and that along with mankind, every animal species serves as part of the Earth's ecosystem.

In communicating with deer, I felt a gentleness unlike any other and gained the insight that their purpose is to hold gentleness—to be gentleness—for man and the Earth. While tuning in to alligators at a zoo one day, I was shocked to feel slightly drunk in their ecstasy of the Earth's subtle swaying—that they could perceive the minutest shift in the Earth's energy. In connecting with whales, I have been moved to tears when feeling their otherworldly spiritual essence that they long to enlighten us with. And horses, too, I learned, have something special to teach us.

As I tuned in one afternoon to Sam, my friend Eve's horse, I was awed, as if I was in the presence of a Dalai Lama-type being. As I opened myself to what Sam wanted to tell me, he said he had been a horse in many lifetimes. As far as he was concerned, it was the best animal body to have. Sam embodied Horse. When I asked him to tell me about Horse, he said, "We are a collective consciousness in and of itself. We are honor. We are forgiveness and forgiving. We hold the wisdom to which all is unfolded, but like the sages of old, must keep it a secret so that you [meaning man] are drawn to us. In us you find yourselves. You find what you have lost—the honor of each other necessary for harmony and the recognition of Oneness of a collective consciousness. We bring you joy. Although we sometimes bring out the ugliness in you [meaning abuse], it must be brought out to be seen, looked at, examined, and healed. This is the only way for change [enlightenment] to occur. We are proud beings. Everything we do and stand for we do with utmost pride [with this he sent images of work and war horses]. Our fondness for man is innate, and we serve as a gateway to your enlightenment of Self. We not only hold the energy of a collective consciousness of Horse, but we also serve as agents to uphold the collective Oneness that isn't felt by you.

We will always hold the space of collective conscious-ness for man because we are Horse and it is so."

The spiritual learnings I received from animals made me wonder if animals are more spiritually evolved than man. But then it dawned on me that when intuitively communicating with any being, the connection is purely a spiritual one. Since I didn't communicate with people this way, I began to see how limiting my physical and men-tal communication with people actually was. I believed that the spiritual Self of every person has deep wisdom too—just the same, of course, as animals. Ultimately the epiphany struck—if all people had unrecognized spiritual wisdom, then that meant I did too . . . hmm . . . Animals were indeed teaching me.

Experiencing the wealth of the spiritual wisdom of animals made me shudder to think of life on this planet without them. Imagine, just for a moment, a world with only humans. It's simply too wretched to imagine.

~

I also learned that animals can have a specific purpose for being in their people's lives. In Charlie's case, besides being my mirror, I intuited that his purpose was to be my spiritual muse—to awaken me to forces greater than myself and/or inside myself. Toby's purpose was to teach me methods of healing. With my two boys supporting me, I still felt the shaky vulnerability when stretching my comfort zones to reach deeper awareness, but doing it with and for them seemed the most natural and only thing to do.

After I had more experience with animal communi-cation, I grew increasingly curious about the nature of

Me with "the Boys" (Charlie has on the darker scarf, Toby the white)

telepathy. How does it really work? Could I find answers to something so nebulous?

"I wouldn't delve into the how's and why's of telepathy," an animal communicator colleague cautioned me.

"Why not?" I asked.

"Because it's not an intellectual thing," she said. "Don't make it one. Aren't you afraid you'll get confused?"

"A little" I said. "But I know my mind won't rest until I get a deeper understanding about it. I need to know how telepathy works. What is the source of this information and by what means does it come through?"

"Well," she said. "I don't want to know how it works, I'm just glad it does!"

I pored through *The Complete Idiot's Guide to Understanding Einstein*, researched metaphysical explanations, and then, thoroughly confused, fled to my longtime friend and spiritual mentor, Ishwar. I knew he was the only one who could untangle the jumble of information for me and I looked forward to what I knew could be a lengthy and intellectually challenging conversation.

"Help me make sense of what telepathy is!" I implored.

"Okay. First, tell me what you think it is," he said with sparkling, curious eyes.

"Well," I sighed, "the definition of telepathy is 'feeling at a distance,' which as I understand it means that you can perceive the essence of any being, whether they're in front of you or on the other side of the world. And this can be done because somehow we're all connected, right?"

"Right. Go on," he said.

"But by what means are we really all connected?" I said, perched at the edge of my chair. "I don't really understand how a telepathic 'feeling' is perceived. How does the transfer of a perception happen? And where is the 'distance' of 'feeling at a distance'?"

"Okay," Ishwar said, delight flickering in his eyes, like there was nothing better in the whole world to talk about. "Let's take it one step at a time. What's your first question?"

"Well, I guess it would be . . . How does telepathy work?"

"First of all," he said, clearing his throat. "Because our attention is so focused on our physical bodies and this physical world, our tendency is to forget our spiritual Self—which is our true Self. Although all beings appear separate, the truth is, we're are connected."

"All beings. You mean animals included, right?" I asked.

"Yes. All living things," he replied. "All beings possess a non-physical, non-visible, non-tangible dimension that suffuses the physical body, and extends beyond it. This non-physical, invisible, intangible dimension is all-pervasive—meaning there is no emptiness, vacuum, or void between any living thing. Telepathy, or intuitive communication, is merely tapping into, or putting your awareness in this other dimension."

"So this non-physical dimension is how and why intuitive communications are innate in all of us?"

He nodded.

"And," I continued, "this is how animals and humans are connected and how animal communication is possible?"

"Correct."

"So here's the next question: What is the non-physical dimension?"

"Consciousness," he answered simply. "Which flows through us by the two non-physical bodies that overlap the physical body, which you've heard me call the astral and causal bodies. Other people may refer to these bodies as something else, but my teacher called them the astral and causal, so that's what I call them."

"And the astral body is the sensory body and the causal body is the one that houses thoughts, right?" I added.

"Correct. The astral, or sensory body, is where all sensory perceptions—meaning the five senses—are experienced. Through the astral body, all sensory perceptions filter into the physical body and consequently, are felt in the physical body."

"So this would explain the feelings or perceptions of 'feeling at a distance'?"

"Yes."

"But does all telepathy or intuitive communication come from the astral body or astral level?"

"Yes. Again, the astral body is the sensory body and telepathy happens because we perceive a feeling and generate the translation."

"Generate a translation?" I asked. "I don't get it."

"You generate the translation into language but the message comes from the sensory, feeling, astral body. Telepathy is the combination of the astral and physical process of communication through ether."

"Through ether . . . because there's no vacuum or void."

"Right."

"Okay," I said. "So what about direct thoughts, or what seem to be direct thoughts, from an animal? Do they come from the astral, sensory body, or the causal, mental body?"

"All intuitive communication comes from the astral, sensory body—even direct thoughts that are received. The causal, mental body houses thoughts, beliefs, and attitudes which are imprinted on the astral body, which are then felt by you and translated into language. Does this make sense?"

"Yeah," I sighed. "But it's a mind twister!"

"It is a mind twister," he laughed. "But from my experience, it's the truth."

"Okay. Next question. What about the 'distance' in 'feeling at a distance'?"

"Actually, there is no 'distance' since we are connecting with what is right here with us, everywhere, all the time. In the dimension of consciousness, or Spirit, where telepathy originates, spatial constraints do not exist."

"Hmmm . . . " I said, letting it all soak in. "So, to us, it just seems like there's distance because our attention is only on the physical. But telepathy is an expansion of our awareness in the non-physical consciousness that exists in everything as One."

"Right. But always remember that while it's fine to feed both the intellect and expand intuition, you must keep them separate. The mind will only get in the way with intuitive communication. Don't forget that."

"Yeah, the mind is pret-ty darn tricky that way, eh? This is a lot to take in. And this is only the beginning of understanding all of this!" I laughed.

"But it's a good beginning," Ishwar beamed back at me.

The conversation with Ishwar spurred my curiosity about the non-physical dimensions. I yearned deeply to experience them, only I didn't know how. I knew that meditation practice was one way, but I was too impatient to sit in mediation for weeks or years to get the insights I wanted.

There was one other thing I didn't know how to do. Although the eternal "what if" worrier in me had subsided somewhat, when it came to Charlie, I was a lost cause. What if he got sick and I couldn't help him? What if he needed me and I couldn't communicate with him? What if he died? Could I communicate with him then? What if I couldn't cope? What if, what if . . .

The most crippling fears are of the unknown. But my fears would soon become known.

Tales of Whales

One snowy afternoon in early January while I cuddled Charlie, he said, "Mom, my contract is up."

Contract? What did he mean? His life contract? Would he soon be dying? Could he know this? Or did he mean he didn't want to be a healer anymore—that his time as my spiritual teacher was finished? Whatever the case, I didn't want to know. I just hugged him tighter.

It was ten days later when he coughed in the night. Consequently, the lung mass was discovered.

We didn't know if it was cancer.

"Let's give it three months," suggested my veterinarian, Dr. Pat. "Then we'll do follow-up X-rays. If there is no change, most likely it will mean it's benign. But if the mass grows, or if there are any additional masses, then in all likelihood, it would mean cancer. So, in the meantime, let's hope for the best."

So that's what I did—hoped and prayed for the best. Charlie was eating well and was his playful, loving, protective self. He seemed fine.

I never asked him anything about the mass during this time. My coping strategy was keeping my head buried in the sand.

~

In February, to help get my mind off my worries about Charlie during this wait-and-see period, I left Charlie and Toby in Steve's doting hands and flew to the Dominican Republic to swim with humpback whales. The trip, facilitated by Penelope Smith, was aboard a ninety-foot catamaran that was one of only three licensed boats legally permitted to bring people out into the ocean to actually swim with these awesome beings. We would be spending a week in the Silver Bank, a hundred-square-mile humpback calving and mating ground eighty miles off the coast of Puerto Plata.

I felt drawn to whales because during an exercise in Penelope's advanced courses, I experienced the essence of Whale. The profound sense of nurturing I received from Whale left me sobbing like a lost child finally safe in her mother's loving arms. I wasn't the only one—I had read many accounts of people being uplifted and changed by whale encounters. What was it about these beings that could touch the heart and Spirit of so many? And why did I and many others find the humpback song so deeply haunting?

I knew that being in close proximity with whales would be profoundly moving—even transformative, I hoped. Maybe this would help me gain more awareness of whatever was going on with Charlie. I needed strength to cope with whatever was in store for us.

As I prepared for the trip, trying to pack the proper gear and clothes, I also did a little reading on whales. I learned about their mysterious evolution—it is believed that fifty million years ago, they were four-legged, wolf-like land mammals. Perhaps they preferred hunting near or in the water and eventually became amphibious, meaning they lived both on land and in water. Then over time, their front legs evolved into fins, their hind legs disappeared, they lost their fur, developed nostrils on the top of their heads, and thus became cetaceans, or ocean mammals. I also read that shamanic lore regards whales as the record keepers. But of what?

To answer my questions, I meditated to recordings of humpback whale songs and received these answers: Whales are the record keepers of the evolution of mankind—they are man's evolutionary grandparents who have held us and watched us evolve. Whales hold infinite love and compassion for mankind despite the cruel slaughtering they have suffered through whaling. And it is their song that is the thread of all life. The resonance of their song holds the essence of Divine Truth, which surrounds us like a web.

I was giddy with excitement to have the chance to swim with these beings.

On February 2, 2002, twenty-two of us boarded the *Bottom Time II* for our whale adventure. After dinner the crew told us that the four-hour crossing early the next morning to the Silver Bank could potentially be very rough. They cautioned that anyone prone to seasickness should take medication before going to bed. But I wasn't worried. I never got seasick. I was proud of my strong sea legs. Being the daughter of a Fort Lauderdale yacht broker and having spent my childhood and teenage summers on the tempestuous waters of Lake Erie, I had been on lots of boats, big and small, and had experienced rough seas on many occasions. The one and only time I had been seasick was as a teenager, when my father, brother, and I got caught in the tail end of a hurricane while bringing a boat back to Fort Lauderdale from the Bahamas. Barring a hurricane, I knew I'd be fine. Just fine.

That night, the gentle rocking of the boat was heavenly and I slept well. I woke when I felt the boat slowly slip out into calm seas at 6:15 the next morning. Cozily curled up in my bunk, I contemplated going up on deck but decided to go back to sleep. Suddenly, the panicked voice in my head, the one I'd managed to keep sequestered, shoved its way up, front and center, bellowing: *Do you know how dangerous this trip is? Those whales could kill you! You haven't snorkeled in years! You're afraid of deep water! What ARE you doing?* I rolled over, pulled the sheet over my head, and willed the voice to return to its exile. It was obviously too late to turn back now.

Minutes later, as the boat effortlessly gained speed, I was gripped with a sudden overwhelming sense of queasiness. I dashed to the back deck. By 6:30 I had twice given the ocean the contents of my stomach. At some point during this four-hour I-would-rather-die-than-feel-this-way crossing, I had an interesting insight. Time and time again as I flung myself over the railing (making sure I wasn't up or downwind of the other half dozen green-faced, fellow barfers), I wondered if there was more to this purging. Towards the end, as my body continued to be wracked with violent dry heaves, I wondered . . . what was I trying to expel? Was it the fear of the unknown of this trip? Was it the fear of losing Charlie? Or something else?

Relief doesn't begin to express my feeling of finally reaching the calm waters of the Silver Bank. While mooring, the captain announced that our crossing had been one of the smoothest in years. Groans reverberated throughout the back deck.

After our stomachs calmed down and we ate what little lunch we were able, we sat on the sun deck and delighted in our surroundings—nothing but the shimmery sea and blue sky as far as we could see. The relaxing, hot tropical sun and light breeze enlivened us from our ordeal.

"Well, I feel a bit brought back to life," I said, and offered my face to the sun.

"Yeah, me, too," said a fellow passenger (and barfer). "And I gotta say one thing—that crossing gave a whole new meaning to sharing a meal with friends!"

"Yeah! Nothing like jockeying for position at the railing to bond in friendship!" someone else said.

"You actually made it to the railing?!" another said, laughing.

"Hey!" said someone else, pointing to the other two licensed boats that had just arrived and anchored within a half mile or so, "You think their passengers fed the fish like we did?"

All joking aside, my purging must have helped exorcise that panicky voice, because it never returned with such insistence.

"Okay, folks!" said the captain over the loudspeaker. "It's time for a swim so you can try your gear. The crew will be waiting for you on the back deck if you need help."

We squeezed ourselves into our wetsuits, donned our snorkel gear, and swam around the boat to make sure we were comfortable. Much to my relief, I discovered that snorkeling is like riding a bike—you don't forget how to do it. And the depth of the water, which was so deep I couldn't even imagine where the bottom was, didn't bother me. I was too mesmerized by the vibrant shades of the ocean's aqua blues and hypnotized by the sunlight that filtered through the water, making glittering spirals that danced down endlessly. These dancing spirals seemed to beckon me to discover where they led . . . as if they could reveal the secrets of the ocean or of Truth.

Having made friends with the ocean and with my gear, I was ready. We split into groups and boarded the two inflatable Zodiacs and were off.

To my dying day, I will remember my first whale encounter. A mother and baby stayed close to our Zodiac for a long time, circling us. The baby kept raising its eye out of the water to get a good look at us. The mamma would blow out a strong, loud, high spout and then the baby would spout an adorable little "ffffftttt." This closeness to us, the captain told us, was a sign that it was all right to get into the water with them. As instructed, we gently slipped into the water so as not to disturb them and floated on the surface in quiet respect. (Swimming toward or after a whale or attempting to reach out to touch it was strictly forbidden.) Mother and baby were about fifteen feet away, face to face with us. The baby floated above its mother, looking at us with intense curiosity. For a few seconds my heart pounded with fear as I realized how vulnerable and tiny I was compared to them. But an instant later all fear vanished as I felt pulled into a dreamlike state, totally transfixed and overwhelmed by a loving, welcome feeling from them. It enveloped and penetrated me on such a deep level that I floated in a surreal, timeless state, like forever in a second. And in me, a long-lost soul memory was desperately calling out to them, expressing that, in their presence, I was finally Home. They swam right toward us, turned, and with utmost grace and swift, effortless movement, were gone. Watching them swim away, my body pulsed with a desperate, frantic urge to scream, "DON'T GO!" Instead, an uncontrollable, primal cry erupted from my throat, but came from the deepest depths of my being.

I bobbed on the surface, dazed. I felt transported, not quite sure what had just happened.

That evening, I was still reeling from the experience. The intense "Home" feeling I had felt from the whales was as though the whole of my being had been witnessed by pure compassion. It was an extraordinarily beautiful feeling but it left me feeling raw, naked, and precariously vulnerable. I felt knocked off guard, unsettled, and frightened.

In discussing this with Penelope, she said, "Don't try to figure it out. Just be with it. You're in Whale Soup. You're being cracked open. The whales will do that. Just let it happen."

"O-kay . . . " I sighed, hesitatingly. Even though I had hoped this trip would bring transformation, I hadn't thought it would be such a challenge. I began to see that while I had boarded the boat with a neatly packed suitcase, I'd been unaware of the utter disarray of my emotional baggage.

I wasn't the only one going through deep shifts. Every night after dinner Penelope led a group sharing. Sometimes we basked in the beauty of another's experience and sometimes we needed to support one another as we navigated our deeply emotional personal insights.

"Whale essence often brings forth emotional issues that need healing," Penelope explained. "The whales want us to wake up spiritually, and our emotional blocks are what keep us from being like them—our true spiritual selves."

My insights unfolded as our whale encounters continued the next day. Before coming on this trip, I had realized that Charlie's protectiveness was a reaction to my fear of being unable to take care of myself. Now, in this new vulnerable state, I was able to recognize that the depth of my fears and anxieties ran much deeper than I'd previously been aware of. No wonder I couldn't mellow out. No wonder I'd always been so driven. I was too occupied with trying to control everything in my path so I would feel safe. Ironically, my biggest fear was facing my fears. Yet I was sick of being boxed in by them, having them dictate my life, keeping me in my comfort zones. Thank God I was in the sanctuary of the ocean, the whales, and a group of accepting people, where I could just hang out and "be," where it was safe to be cracked open, vulnerable, and start healing.

My paramount fear was of losing Charlie. What eluded me was the root cause of why the mere thought of losing him sent me into such deep despair. Yes, I loved him deeply and didn't want to be without him, but there was something else—something I wouldn't discover until months later.

Seeing the depth of my fearfulness led me also to an insight about Charlie's protectiveness. A veterinary technician had once described his behavior as "fear barking," which, at the time, I didn't understand. Now I did. Charlie, just like me (though not timid), was fearful in general and hid it well. In his moments of barking frenzy dog aggression, although he was partly carrying out what he considered to be his canine duty of protecting me, he was trying to control his environment to feel safe. No wonder he was especially set off by dogs his size or larger—he was simply afraid of them. Now I finally understood him and hoped that in my becoming less anxious, he would too.

~

The day before leaving the Silver Bank I had one last unforgettable whale encounter. Our group floated above an adolescent whale with its mamma. The mamma stayed below us while the adolescent circled us close to the surface several times, curiously and intently taking us all in. While it made its last unhurried circle around us, I gazed into its eye. I had heard that gazing into the eye of a whale is like seeing into or being seen by God. For me, this was also true. It was like being swaddled in an all-encompassing Compassion, as if nothing but Love existed. And for those few transcendent moments, nothing else did. It was as though every intricate secret of creation was being tenderly whispered to my soul—and the only "secret" was Love.

The lasting affect of this encounter brought me the gift of tranquility as I had never felt before. Although I still had much growth ahead of me in dealing with my anxieties, I was no longer fretting as much about the road ahead. And for the first time in my life, I felt a lightening of my emotional armor. I realized I didn't need to be so defensive, or be ever-alert on emotional guard duty—I could, at least, go on break.

The last night at sea, under a star-swept sky, I sat alone on the deck, staring out into the blackness of the ocean. I let my body sway with the slow, gentle rocking of the boat. As cool breezes brushed my neck and face, I wrapped my shawl tight around me. I felt like a chrysalis about to come out of its cocoon. I had asked for transformation and now my wings were forming. As I sat marveling at the beauty of the night, something I realized I didn't do often enough, I wondered what the moon and night sky looked like to the whales. The whales! Gratefulness poured from my heart out to them.

As I sat there, I asked them how to integrate all of my experiences. The message came quickly and concisely: "Don't think. Feel."

My mind started to shoot back with, "What do you mean by . . . ?" but stopped. "Got it," I told them. "Don't think. Feel."

I understood they wanted me to continue to feel them in my heart. Earlier in the week I had such intense longing to see them that I was practically in a tizzy if I thought I might miss even one potential encounter. I understood I had placed too much importance on the actual physical encounters, and they were simply asking that I feel their loving presence and carry this with me. I understood, too, that they wanted me to notice my excessive emphasis on the physical realm in general. They wanted me to gain deeper awareness of the higher aspects, or realms of the nonphysical—they wanted me to experience these realms. And I also understood that this awareness of the nonphysical would help me with Charlie . . . that such awareness would help me detach from my desperate fear of losing him. Exactly how I would get this awareness, I didn't know.

The next day, as we left the Silver Bank, we watched for our whale friends. Just as the whale grounds were almost out of sight, we saw a whale slap its pectoral fin on the surface over and over again. We laughed through our tears at this symbolic goodbye.

≈

Another parting gift I received from the whales was giving myself permission to not be "mainstream." My need for the acceptance of friends and family was so strong that

I had dismissed my true self in trying to fit into the norm. Never, in my entire life, had I ever fit into the norm, and I'd always been ashamed of this, feeling myself to be a misfit. But after being with the whales and other like-minded passengers, for the first time in my life I no longer felt I had to try to squeeze myself into shoes that didn't fit. Finally I was able to give myself permission to be me. I was coming home in my truth.

~

With all the shifts and discoveries I had made on this trip, clarity about Charlie's condition still eluded me. After the boat docked, I asked Penelope to briefly tune in to him to see what he had to say.

Sitting beside her, I watched as she leaned her elbow on the table in front of her, put her chin in her hand, and briefly closed her eyes. "I see what he's doing," she said. "He's a very aware being. He has known about the lung mass for quite a while. He says he's in control of it—only he can shrink it or make it grow, so there's nothing you or anyone can do. He doesn't want you to worry. This wait-and-see time is his way of getting you used to the idea that he won't be around forever." She paused. "Anything else you want to know?" she asked me.

"No, not now. I need to digest this. Thank you."

"Please keep in touch. Let me know how he is," she said.

I was profoundly touched that Charlie would give me this chance to slowly adjust to the inevitability of his death.

Hearing Charlie say not to worry and that he was in control of his tumor was uplifting. I assumed that he would choose to stick around and spend more time with me. Nonetheless, panic crept inside me. And now, a new question began to nag at me like a pesky mosquito I couldn't swat—could Charlie really choose to stay or go? Could any being?

Because of You, I Am

Prayer and Surrender

The next month I debated when to take Charlie in for follow-up X-rays. Dr. Pat had said three months, but I kept procrastinating because I just couldn't face it.

"You should have the X-rays done soon," one voice would say.

"But he's fine," another voice rebutted. "He acts completely healthy and normal."

And on it went. I cancelled one veterinary appointment after another as my indecision raged. But one afternoon in March while snuggling Charlie, I heard a strong intuitive voice say, "There's something you need to know." To this day I'm unsure if the message came from Charlie or my intuition, but I immediately made an appointment at the specialty clinic for the following week.

A couple of days before the appointment, Charlie's mouth was bloody after eating his dinner. Looking and feeling in his mouth, I found a small, nickel-sized bloody lump in the gum line above an upper right molar. I was only mildly alarmed, but relieved I had made the appointment. I was sure the lump was nothing and could be easily removed. I thought that while removing this lump, they could clean his teeth too, since he had stopped chewing on his toothbrush a few months before. I just assumed he'd lost interest in brushing his teeth, and I hadn't questioned it. I'd also noticed in the past months that his breath was foul, but attributed this to his needing his teeth cleaned.

During our appointment, I got so caught up in discussing the chest X-rays that I almost forgot to mention the lump in Charlie's mouth.

"Oh, and I discovered this the other night," I said in an offhand manner. I pulled Charlie's lip up, exposing the lump to Dr. Harlington.

"From the looks of this," he said, rubbing his hand over it, "it might be a melanoma. It's black, which means it might be malignant. If it is, then it's possible that the lung mass is malignant too."

I was dumbfounded.

"Melanoma sometimes starts in the mouth and spreads to the lungs," he continued. "And his foul breath could also be a sign of oral malignancy. We'll do a biopsy of the lump."

"I-I had no idea that it could potentially be so serious," I said.

"Well, we won't know anything until we do the biopsy. Are you going to wait in the lobby?" he asked.

"Yes."

"I'll let you know as soon as we're finished," he said.

I leaned down and gave Charlie a kiss on the nose. "I'll see you in a little while," I told him. Charlie looked impatient—like he just wanted to get this over with.

I handed the leash to Dr. Harlington. "C'mon, Sir Charles," he said. "Let's see if there's anybody out here to bark at."

Charlie strutted out of the room, eager for an adventure.

I walked zombie-like into the lobby. Was this really happening?

I called Steve.

"Melanoma?" he said in disbelief.

"I should've known something was wrong," I said. "He hasn't wanted to brush his teeth for weeks. I just thought he'd lost interest."

"I did, too," Steve said.

"I should've known to look in his mouth," I said. "And you know how he's been preferring soft food lately. I should've known! And his bad breath—he's only had that a couple of months. Oh, God, I feel so guilty!"

"Me, too," Steve said. "But it's not our fault—either of us, so don't go blaming yourself. Yes, maybe we should have known. But maybe it's not malignant. There are too many maybes. Let's get the results and we'll go from there. Call me as soon as you know anything."

I grabbed a *Ladies' Home Journal* from the table and mindlessly flipped through the pages. I continued to chastise myself and prayed that it wasn't cancer and for strength if it was. I was so deep into my self-flagellation that I jumped when I heard Dr. Harlington's voice.

"Mary Ann?"

I searched his face for a clue of the test results but it revealed nothing.

"The oral biopsy showed malignancy," he said, without emotion.

Malignancy . . . I felt as though I'd been paralyzed by a poison dart.

"The X-rays showed that the lung mass has only slightly enlarged," he continued. "There are no other visible masses, which means that the oral malignancy may not have spread to the lungs."

"H-how can we be sure?" I asked, finally finding my voice.

"Well, we can't. What I recommend is to take Charlie to Madison, Wisconsin. The University of Wisconsin School of Veterinary Medicine is one of the top veterinary cancer treatment centers in the U.S. They can do more extensive tests there. And they're doing a vaccine trial for melanoma. So maybe Charlie could be included in the trial."

"Is there any other treatment we can do?"

"No, not really," he said. "The type of melanoma Charlie has does not respond well to chemotherapy or radiation. Unfortunately, I think the vaccine trial is your only option."

"How do we get an appointment?"

"I'll call and set it up for you and let you know. Let's hope for the best, okay?"

"Okay," I said fighting back tears.

"I'm sorry. Call me and let me know how it goes."

As we drove home, Charlie was still slightly groggy from the sedation but sat tall and proud in the back seat, taking everything in. While we were stopped at a traffic light, a man in the car next to us had the audacity to look over at us, and Charlie barked at him with his usual bark that seemed to say, "Hey, what the heck are you lookin' at, buddy?!"

"Yeah! You tell him!" I laughed, instead of getting exasperated. I kind of wanted to bark at the guy myself—just to see what it felt like. I laughed again at Charlie as he postured and scanned the intersection for another candidate to bark at. But just underneath the surface of my laughter, I could feel the tears bubbling to the surface, awaiting their turn.

Several days later, Steve, Charlie, Toby, and I were off to Madison.

While we waited for Charlie's assessment to be completed, Steve and I slowly walked Toby around the veterinary school grounds. The strain of being on tenterhooks left us lost in our own thoughts. It was a cold March day but the sun shone brightly and as I lifted my face up to take in its warmth, peacefulness washed through me. I felt Toby tug on his leash and looked down to see him sniffing around a bush. Just under it was a plaque that read:

> If tears could build a stairway
> And memories a lane
> I'd walk right up to Heaven
> And bring you home again

Tears streamed down my cheeks. Staring at the plaque, I prayed, I begged, for the only thing I knew to ask for—acceptance—of whatever happened.

"Well, I've got good news and bad news," said Dr. Alexi, who was the head of the vaccine trial. "The good news is that I've accepted Charlie into the trial."

Steve and I glanced at each other with relief.

"But the bad news," he continued, his face regretful, "is why I accepted him. Charlie's X-rays showed another tumor in his lungs. The melanoma has spread."

I felt Steve's hand squeeze mine.

Dr. Alexi put the X-rays on the screen and pointed to a second, smaller lung mass.

"Why didn't this show up in the X-rays at the specialty clinic?" I asked disbelievingly.

"We have better equipment here," said Dr. Alexi.

"Right," I said, "Dr. Harlington did mention that." I reached for a tissue on the counter. I knew any second I'd be needing it.

"So where do we go from here?" Steve asked.

"Well, this type of melanoma," Dr. Alexi said, "typically starts in the mouth or toes and spreads to the lungs. Often, by the time it's discovered, it's too late. The purpose of the vaccine is to build up Charlie's immune system so that his body literally eats up the cancer. But here's what you need to understand. The goal of the trial is not to hope for a cure. The goal is to hope for a remission so that Charlie will live long enough to die of something else."

"What's your success rate?" I asked.

"Most of the dogs in the trial are doing well. Some have been cancer-free for some time and others are showing signs of remission. And then, of course, we've had a few who haven't made it," he paused. "So would you like to put Charlie in the trial? If you need some time to think about it, I can—"

Steve and I shared a knowing look. "No," I interrupted. "We don't need time to think. We'll do it."

We left the veterinary school with renewed hope. Charlie would need to return to Madison for the first dose while the remaining eight doses would be administered by my regular vet, Dr. Pat, over a thirteen-week period.

Our drive home from Madison that evening was somber. Steve drove while Toby co-piloted from his coveted spot in the front passenger seat. I cradled Charlie in my lap in the back. I hugged and kissed him and sang every "Charlie" song I could think of—"When You Wish Upon A Star," "The Impossible Dream," and a host of goofy made-up songs I'd sung to him since his puppyhood. I savored the feel of his soft, velvety fur, and breathed in his comforting, sweet, Charlie smell—a smell Steve described as "salve for the soul." I thought about our life together and tried to be positive. I knew nothing was in my control. No matter how desperately I wanted him to stay, I realized that his living longer might not be in his—or my—highest good. So I asked God to rid me of the selfishness of wanting to keep him with me. Then I remembered the whales and how they wanted me to increase my awareness of the nonphysical realms. But I didn't know how to do this. Ultimately there was only one thing to do—surrender.

A few days later, I watched Charlie prance around the backyard, patrolling for birds to chase away, when it dawned on me that I had made the decision about putting him in the vaccine trial without even asking him if it was what he wanted.

"Come here!" I said, stepping outside. He bounded over, then stopped to give a quick warning woof! at a flock of geese flying overhead.

"How dare they fly in your airspace! But you told 'em, didn't you!"

He looked at me and wagged his tail proudly.

I kneeled down and received some good ol' Charlie kisses. We sat on the patio and I twirled his long, curly ears through my fingers. Mentally, I projected the vaccine process to him and said, "I want to do it because it's the only thing we can do. And it's a chance for you to live longer."

I could feel that he was okay with it—mostly because I wanted it. I could feel that he just wanted to enjoy his life and didn't want anything invasive. He wasn't worried about a thing. Sure wish I could've said the same for myself!

With the sobering cancer diagnosis, and whether or not the vaccine proved effective, I had to pull my head out of the sand, at least for a little while, and acknowledge that Charlie's death was somewhere on the horizon. I thought about the losses of other animal companions, close family members, and my best friend. This time it was Charlie—my surrogate child—the being who had given me more love, comfort, emotional healing, and understanding than any other being in my life. I was angered at my impotence in understanding death and I begged God to give me a deeper spiritual understanding of it. Otherwise, I didn't know how I'd cope when Charlie's time came. My one consolation, I reminded myself, was that I could connect with Charlie after he died. But could I? What if my emotional attachment or grief hindered me from communicating with him? I knew it would be possible for other animal communicators to do so, but *I* wanted to. I cursed the insidious doubt that was provoking fear in my heart. I had to get some answers . . . somehow.

Tales of Whales Continued

One day, before Charlie's cancer diagnosis, I was putting a book away and a folded piece of paper fell out. On it was a list of my totem animals that I had written down prior to the whale trip. Totem animals are those that emulate a person's nature, potential, or challenges. One "chooses" them randomly from a deck of cards, each illustrated with a different animal. The person selects one animal for each direction—north, south, east, west, above, and below. Reading this forgotten paper gave me goosebumps. My totem animal to the west was Whale. According to the book that accompanied the deck of cards, the animal to the west "guides you to your personal truth and inner answers. It also shows you the path to your goals."

I had indeed received many inner answers and personal truths from the whales. But now the answers I wanted most were about the spiritual process of death itself. What really happens to beings when they die? Where do we go exactly? These questions were burning in me. I needed answers. I needed to *know*. I needed the whales.

~

With Steve's blessing, I planned another trip to the Dominican Republic.

"But I'm so torn about going again," I told him. "I hate missing Charlie's first vaccine. Now that I know it's cancer, I hate being away."

"I know. But he'll be with me so you don't need to worry."

Even as we drove to the airport, I wasn't sure I was doing the right thing.

"You have to go," Steve said. "You have to do this for yourself. Whatever answers you get will help Charlie, me, *and* Toby."

So off I went with a heavy heart but a clearer conscience.

Knowing that Penelope would be there lessened my anxieties. I knew I could depend on her guidance to help me deal with Charlie's condition.

At the last minute, however, Penelope couldn't come. Her beloved Afghan Hound, Reya, was dying and Penelope needed to be with her. There it was. Penelope herself was going through the very thing I had hoped she could help *me* cope with. But believing there is a reason for everything, I searched inside myself for the lesson the Universe was giving me. I grumbled at the answer I received—it appeared it was time for me to quit relying on others and lean on myself.

Since the group in February had been a close, congenial one, I assumed this group would be the same and looked forward to the camaraderie of my fellow passengers. But although everyone seemed nice, I felt I didn't fit in. I realized this was a reflection of what was going on inside me. Again, I grumbled at the Universe's message— that the purpose of the trip was not to connect with the group or anyone in it, but to connect with myself—and that the only place I needed to fit in was inside me.

This time I fared better on the crossing to the Silver Bank with only dreadful queasiness. No trips to the railing were required. But the next day was different. Feeling ill with flu-like symptoms, I decided to stay behind on the main boat. I waved goodbye from the upper deck as my fellow passengers excitedly went off in the Zodiacs. I spent the day in my cabin in a meditative/wakeful/dreamlike state, connecting with the whales. The whales conveyed to me that the physical body—or physical experience—is such a miniscule part of life and the big picture. I sensed the higher realms that pulsed and radiated through these great beings and understood that their otherworldliness and connection to these higher realms is part of their mysterious essence that draws us to them. I felt as though I was being bathed in vast levels of consciousness that were connected with each other, yet were one. I became aware, too, of the connection of these realms to the physical—that because of these higher realms this physical world appears real. In feeling the vastness of these other realms, I understood the physical experience as being a mere blip of the Whole.

With this, it became clear to me that all other realms/dimensions are right here with us, right now, all the time—and that man, too, is multidimensional. We think that only the physical exists because we feel limited to our physical senses of what we see, hear, touch, taste, and feel. But if man were not multidimensional, then how could we perceive intuitions or intuitive communications? How could I have perceived the otherworldly, nonphysical realms the whales were showing me if I were not multidimensional myself? Though it seems that we are physical beings who happen to be multidimensional, in truth, as the whales showed me, we are able to manifest as physical beings *because* we are multidimensional.

Although I received only an elusive impression of these other levels of consciousness, I did, in a timeless way, experience them as more real than the physical. Then, as these realms instantly faded into a dreamlike memory, the whales conveyed the message, "There is no death."

Then what *does* happen? I ached for the answer.

But I received no further information. It was as if this was the end of the lesson—for now. But it stuck with me. The way they showed me how the *non*-physical aspect of life is a more important aspect of being, they had gotten my attention!

And so I began to question the nature of conscious-ness. What is it? I searched my memory for the many times I'd heard Ishwar explain this. Then, when I least expected it, the answer came, swirling inside me, whis-pering, "Awareness!"

That was it—Awareness! Consciousness is awareness!

But . . . awareness of *what?*

The same intuitive swirling again whispered the answer. "Energy . . . Being . . . Being energy beings."

Now it was beginning to make some sense. I now had some experiential knowledge of the vast levels of consciousness that I had simply heard and read about. I had experienced that these levels were separate yet all connected. And I was left with the understanding that *everything*—all physical bodies *and* this material world—exists only because Consciousness is woven through us.

The next day I was feeling better. "Coincidentally," after I received the message from the whales stressing the importance of the non-physical, our group had an astounding encounter with three whales who stayed with us for five hours. At one point the group of whales grew to five. Even the crew was amazed. They'd never seen anything like it. We cheered and whooped at the whales, which spurred them on to perform for us. They leapt high in the air, in spectacular breach after breach, showing off their athletic prowess as if to express to us how fabulous it was to be a whale. Their pectoral slaps seemed as if they were clapping for themselves and their tail breaches (a sort of tail-first breach) looked like they were playfully mooning us. Every now and then they would "spy-hop"—stick their heads straight out of the water just far enough to get a glimpse of us howling and clapping. Then they would gently glide back into the water. We watched, riveted, to see where they would appear next and what act they would perform. I don't know if we enjoyed them more or they us. We were in and out of the water with them and I lost track of how many eye-to-eye contacts I made with each of them. I felt somehow that this encounter was in celebration of receiving their message—the importance of the *non*-physical—and that this unforgettable get-together was an example of how wonderfully joyous the physical can be *because* we are beings of Consciousness. This day filled my Spirit so deeply that in the ensuing days I was able to understand the spiritual secret of the whales' song.

It is known that humpbacks sing the same song over and over—sometimes for days. Scientists have never discovered the reason for this. When a humpback is singing it appears to be in a meditative state. One amazing characteristic is that they sometimes interrupt their song on one note, and then days, weeks, or even months later, continue singing from the note where they left off. Scientists have also been baffled by the phenomenon of humpbacks having a new song every year. How and why do they do this? Scientists report that only male humpbacks sing and the sole purpose of their singing is for mating.

I knew there had to be more than met the scientific eye. The information I received from the whales was that females sing too. And their song is indeed used as a physical mating ritual. However, I understood that the spiritual meaning of their song is a call of desiring union between the physical and non-physical. It is the most sacred prayer of union with the Divine, of enlightenment. It is of little wonder that some people weep when hearing the song of these amazing beings. Man is being drawn to the very thing which he seeks.

And it was no wonder that I, too, was drawn to them. I was seeking an understanding of death—the deepest mystery of union.

On both trips I had begged the whales to give me the experience of a "singer"—a lone whale in its meditative singing state. On each of the trips I'd taken, some of the passengers had experienced a singer, and it had filled them with exhilaration for days. But each time I had been on the other Zodiac. In this, I learned that all things happen in their own time.

Sometimes when we were out on the Zodiacs and didn't see any whales for a while, the captain would put the hydrophone in the water so we could hear them.

Hearing them "live, in concert" was an awesome cacophony resembling cows mooing, seals barking, and elephants trumpeting all at once. As they chattered away, I sometimes felt like we were eavesdropping on a clandestine meeting. I could sense their discussion of their migration—like a familial sharing—as well as their discussion of oceanic occurrences. I felt that they, much better than we, understood the Earth and how to help her.

From this trip I was beginning to accept that the nonphysical spiritual Self of *any* being is just as real as this physical reality. This insight cracked me open to a spiritual depth I had yearned for my entire life. Step by step, I began feeling my own integration as a physical *and* spiritual being. Not only was I seeking God, but I began feeling myself as a spiritual being seeking to regain the memory of Self.

~

Once again I was happy to return home to my boys. In the weeks following the March whale trip, Charlie was doing well. He was receiving the vaccine, eating normally, enjoying life and, from all appearances, wasn't ill at all. When tuning in to him, he said he sometimes felt sluggish, but was fine. He said he was glad to have the vaccine and was very much at peace. I was the restless, agitated one. Would I receive the answers to my questions about death before his time came?

I implored God, my Spirit Helpers, the Universe, or whoever was listening, for understanding of what happens to a being's life force upon death. I believed in past lives, but where does the life force go, exactly? What did it do? What is the "afterlife," the "other side," or "Heaven"? I refused to ask or pray for answers—I demanded them. One by one they came.

The Shamanic Path

The deeper awareness of death that I longed for came from an unexpected source: shamanism. I learned of an upcoming shamanic workshop in the Chicago area, "Dying and Beyond," sponsored by the Foundation for Shamanic Studies. Having previously taken a basic class in shamanism through the foundation a year earlier, I was eager to view death from the shamanic standpoint. Eagerness, however, could not be used to describe my first introduction to shamanism.

Prior to my discovery of animal communication, anything to do with the Native American culture gave me the creeps. This was because as a child I had frequent recurring nightmares in which I witnessed a violent, bloody attack by native Indians. In this recurring dream, I crouched under a table, peering through a slit in a table covering. I was so terrified by the brutality of bloodshed I witnessed and of being found and hacked up myself that I could barely breathe. The dreams stopped when I was around seven years old, but the terror I experienced from them was so real that I could never get over my fear of and repulsion toward the Native American culture. So the only thing I knew or even cared to know about shamanism was that a shaman is an indigenous medicine man or woman.

Unexpectedly, in the first animal communication course with Penelope, she introduced us to shamanic drumming and "journeying." Had I known this was going to be part of the course I would not have gone. On the first morning of the workshop, Penelope drummed and chanted as we stood around a medicine wheel (a sacred circle to honor the four directions—east, west, north, and south). I closed my eyes in an attempt to calm the shrieking voice in my head saying that this was, indeed, pure unadulterated voodoo. When I opened my eyes, I noticed that everyone else was moving to the drumbeat as if they were actually *enjoying* it. I was stunned. Was I missing something? What the heck was there was to enjoy about this? So I closed my eyes to calm myself. In a striking vision, which probably only lasted a few seconds, I vividly saw Penelope in full native garb with long braids. Seeing and feeling this was so real and felt so natural that it frightened me. My eyes flew open and I was startled, yet relieved, to see Penelope in front of me with short hair and western clothes. Even more surprising was the fact that while having this vision, I felt that I, myself, was a member of an indigenous tribe—it had felt so completely normal and comfortable. Had I been Native American in a past life? No. No way. Not me! Strangely, however, standing in the circle, as each drumbeat pulsed through me, I felt my repulsion of Native Americanism start to fade away. I began to feel transfixed by the beat and then it seemed to be coming from within me instead of from the drums. My mind still wanted to resist all of this but the beat in my body was so powerful—like a power greater than I was at work inside me—and the beat started to shift me from side to side, and I began to move with it. With each beat that coursed through me, I felt layers of myself—long forgotten layers—being peeled off. It was exhilarating! I needed more!

A day or so later, during a meditation in the workshop, I saw, as if watching a movie screen, what felt to be a past life. Although I was watching with some detachment, I totally identified with one of the characters to the extent that I "knew" it was me. In this past life I was a Native American child and my family was slaughtered by another tribe. I witnessed and survived the attack and was adopted by a non-native family who raised me with the belief that any native practice was of the devil. I was raised to not only forget about my heritage but to be ashamed of it. Wanting to be loved by my adopted family and fit in, I disinfected myself of what was natural to me—feeling at one with animals and nature. Although forsaking my heritage made me feel empty and alone, I wanted the safety of being taken care of and feared that if I didn't adhere to my new family's rules, I would be rejected.

It was then that I had the epiphany that my recurring childhood nightmares had actually been the traumatic memory of what had happened in that past life. The nightmares had stopped when I was seven, which was the approximate age at which I was adopted in my Native American past life. Once this was revealed, I felt a deep kinship with the shamanic path and longed to discover more. From that point on in Penelope's workshop, I allowed the drumming to release parts of me that had been yearning to be set free my entire life—and most likely, for many lifetimes. It was euphoric to be set free of chains I hadn't even known existed.

∾

Shamanism is the oldest spiritual practice and form of healing known to man. It is not only indigenous to Native Americans, but to all indigenous cultures throughout the world. One fundamental of shamanism is that all life forms are sacred. Its purpose is to heal and restore balance to all—"all" includes healing of any physical, emotional, or mental condition in humanity as well as healing of animals, nature, and the Earth. The understanding is that healing takes place at the soul level so that the physical body can then balance and heal itself more easily. Historically, in the tribal community, a shaman performed multiple roles: as a healer, seer, storyteller, diviner of information, psychotherapist and conflict resolution worker, interpreter of dreams, healer of the dead (known as psychopomp work, which assists beings when they cross over or helps to heal their unrest), and conductor of ceremonies to honor the life cycles of man and nature.

In her book, *Welcome Home: Life After Healing— Following Your Soul's Journey Home*, Sandra Ingerman, a renowned shaman, states, "Shamanism is a way of accessing spiritual guidance that dates back tens of thousands of years. It is practiced all over the world, in Siberia, Lapland, parts of Asia, Africa, Australia, and North and South America. *Shaman* is a Tungus word meaning 'healer' or 'one who sees in the dark.' A shaman is a man or woman who enters an altered state of consciousness and travels outside time and space into non-ordinary reality, which I think of as a universe parallel to ours."

Today, in large part thanks to the amazing dedicated research and extraordinary work of anthropologist and shaman Michael Harner, founder of the Foundation for Shamanic Studies, shamanism is thriving in many parts of western society. As I have heard Michael Harner say, non-ordinary reality is not fantasy or imagination; it is simply different from our ordinary reality. Our ability to access it can help us in our lives by giving us the same kind of wisdom we have read about from the great mystics and prophets of history.

Shamans walk with equal awareness in both ordinary and non-ordinary realities (or physical and non-physical realms, respectively) and can always distinguish between them. Because of this, it is said that shamans act as liaisons between realities—much the same as the whales, who, in my opinion, are the shamans of the sea.

The shamanic perspective is that all life is connected as One. In other words, nothing (no thing) can be affected without something else, in turn, being affected. This refers not only to humans and animals but also to plants, insects, and even rocks, sand, and indeed all of the Earth itself. All is a part of the Whole.

Accepting rocks and minerals as having Spirits was, at first, a departure for me. But after my experience connecting with the mountain during Penelope's workshop, as well as other occasions of feeling a deep at-one-ment from rocks or the Earth—and receiving grounding and wisdom from them—it is no longer a stretch for me to acknowledge them, and their awareness, as a part of the Whole. Shamans understand empirically that we are all a part of this collective awareness. Through a shamanic journey, which I will explain, we can experience what it is like to be a tree, insect, animal, body of water, or grain of sand if we access this awareness that allows us to feel our oneness.

Shamanically speaking, although illness manifests physically, there is a spiritual reason or lesson associated with it. An illness, be it physical, emotional, or mental, indicates that there is imbalance or disharmony in one's life. The focus of a shaman's healing is not necessarily to bring a cure to an illness (although this can happen), but to restore balance and harmony to the whole being—be it human, animal, or plant.

Spiritual autonomy, or the ability to "see" for oneself in non-ordinary reality, can be achieved by the shamanic journey. I sometimes describe journeying as a form of meditation or prayer. A shaman—or shamanic practitioner—can journey, or enter this state of non-ordinary reality by listening to a repetitive percussive sound, typically a steady drumbeat, which can be live or recorded—both are equally effective. The beat relaxes the body into deep receptive, meditative, trance, or dreamlike states, allowing the shamanic practitioner to journey—or "travel"—into cosmology of non-ordinary reality in order to receive or divine information or healing help. This spiritual autonomy—seeing and experiencing for oneself—is what I have found most engaging about shamanism. Nothing can equal personal spiritual experience. It's the best faith-builder there is.

When in this relaxed, trance-like state, you connect with Compassionate Helping Spirits (or Power Animals) who escort you through the cosmology of non-ordinary reality and provide the spiritual wisdom or healing that is being requested.

When a person journeys, he or she lies down; however, journeying can also be done sitting up. Darkness or an eye cover is used to block out any light so that the journeyer can more easily disengage from this physical ordinary reality. The journeyer will have a specific intent or focus regarding a question to be answered, information to be discovered or clarified, or something to be healed.

The beauty of journeying is that knowledge can be obtained regarding anything. As soon as the drumming begins, the journeyer will state his or her intent, and the journey into non-ordinary reality begins. A journey typically lasts ten to thirty minutes, the end of which is signaled by a change in the drumbeat. The journeyer then returns to ordinary reality with the information or healing help.

I once wanted to know the spiritual explanation for the wasting disease of deer. In my journey I was given an answer—and though it is not an absolute answer, it held significance for me. The answer was this: because man's gentleness toward nature and his fellow humans has so profoundly wasted away, nature's gentlest of creatures are also wasting away. It is up to us to heal our interactions with nature, the Earth, and each other. I realized this as one example of how one thing can affect the Whole. And I realized my part in it. I realized that my gentleness, or lack thereof, toward myself, the Earth, and all other beings had a significant impact in the domino effect of the All.

Through shamanism, my awareness of the Whole was growing. And through the "Dying and Beyond" workshop, I would soon learn that the Whole includes death.

Dying and Beyond

The weekend of the shamanic "Dying and Beyond" workshop was gloriously warm and sunny. I felt the Heavens were warming my heart with hope after a long, dreary winter. As I made the drive, I felt excited, but also anxious. Since I would be driving over two hours round trip each day, I hoped this workshop would be worth my effort and provide me with some answers. I hated to think that I'd be away from my boys for most of the weekend and not gain anything.

I followed the signs to our middle-of-nowhere meeting place in a forest preserve. Just as I arrived, two other participants pulled in. We exchanged hellos and helped each other carry our drums and folding chairs.

Our "meeting room" was a yurt: a cozy, domed, canvas tent approximately thirty feet in diameter with screened windows and wooden floor. After organizing my gear, I stepped outside to enjoy the forest preserve and the glorious spring air. As I breathed in deeply, my entire body relaxed. I could feel the trees and wildflowers rejoicing in awakening from their winter slumber—it was as though they were stretching their leaves and petals out into the world like seasoned yogis. And the birds weren't merely singing—they were belting out their "spring is here!" songs like opera singers trying to upstage one another. Surrounded by this cheerful chorus, I felt enlivened.

But it was almost time to start, so I pulled myself away and headed back. Grabbing a banana from the snack table, I settled in and opened my notepad. Our facilitator and shaman, Myron Eshowsky, began by explaining how shamans view death.

"Shamans believe that when a being dies, it acquires wisdom and/or receives healing in its Spirit form, and then can return in a different physical form."

My heart was already uplifted. This confirmed what I intuitively felt about Charlie. If cancer was to be the vehicle to take him out of his body, he would just be gone for a while to gather wisdom or heal; then, hopefully, he'd be back.

"The shamanic belief," Myron continued, "is that death is not viewed as something 'gone wrong.' It is simply a way to heal. This means that even though the life force is no longer in the body, it continues to exist, healing and growing in the Spirit realms."

Although I had heard this before, now, for whatever reason, I was extremely intrigued.

"So if there are no questions," Myron said, "we'll start right in with our first journey. That's why we're here—for you to get experiential knowledge—not to listen to me talk."

Each journey in the "Dying and Beyond" workshop took me to a deeper awareness. In the initial journeys I was shown that a being continues to heal and grow after death as a result of its experience in a physical life. After dying, the growth sometimes happens at a more accelerated pace.

I was also shown in journeys that, generally speaking, when the life force leaves a physical form, it is not the end of existence but rather a transition to a new, more fulfilling aspect of the being's experience. Sometimes a being must hurry through its lessons and/or purpose of its physical life (meaning a short physical life) to get to other realms where it can flourish and grow. The more meaningful aspects of a being's growth and healing experience sometimes occur after death.

For one journey, we were instructed to go to a friend or family member who had died and see how they were doing. I journeyed to my best friend. During his life, he had dreamt of becoming a concert pianist. Though amazingly talented, he never accomplished this dream. In the journey, I was delighted by how vibrant and happy he was in his new "afterlife"—which felt to me to be just as lifelike as the physical. He looked more or less the same, appearance-wise, only with a regal, spiritually enlightened air. He was overjoyed that I had finally come to visit him and was eager to show me his fabulous new life. He had, indeed, fulfilled his dream and become a famous composer and pianist. I understood that the reason his physical life had been short was because his greater destiny was to expand his talent as a musician in the Spirit realm. He was just about to give a performance, and dedicated the concert to me. His music was not audible but felt. It penetrated through my very core, conveying a love that far surpassed anything I had felt from him when he was alive. I was filled with an ecstatically blissful feeling, and understood that he is still very much with me and loves me the same—maybe even more. I wept tears of joy at having this special time together again. I also understood that his music is not only needed and relished in the Spirit realm, but that someday, through a composer in this physical realm, it will be brought here for our healing. It will be music that will evoke deep feelings and healing in all who hear it, inspiring them to awaken to higher levels of understanding and compassion within themselves.

Now, with these experiences, I more fully understood what the whales meant by "there is no death" and that the physical life is a quick stopover—a miniscule part of the bigger picture.

The afterlife was no longer just a concept to me. I had "seen" and witnessed an afterlife. I was beginning to rest a little easier about what would happen to Charlie when he died. I felt that if he did die of cancer, or whenever he died, for that matter, it was because he had better things awaiting him in the Spirit realm.

Also, it was no longer just a concept that death is simply a shift. From the journeys, I was receiving a visceral understanding that at death the spiritual essence once existing in a physical body simply leaves the physical and carries on in the everlasting, spiritual realms, or non-ordinary reality. As I had experienced in my journey to my best friend, after the shift takes place, the essence of the being itself remains the same. It just no longer has the awareness of the five senses in the physical body. Now I understood that this continued existence of a being's essence is how a medium (a person who communicates with the dead) or an animal communicator can communicate with a person or animal once they have left their physical body.

The workshop journeys also gave me deeper access to spiritual realms that I had only fleetingly glimpsed with the whales. Now I had a more comprehensive understanding of what the whales wanted to teach me—that the "realness" of any given reality is a matter of attention or focus. In the journeys I experienced these realms of non-ordinary reality as more real—more like "Home"—than the physical realm. But after each journey, when I returned to this realm of ordinary reality and regained complete awareness of the five senses, the physical world seemed, once again, to be the only "real" realm. Quite a paradox. The difference was that now I began to accept that both realms—ordinary and non-ordinary reality—are equally real. It's only a matter of where I place my attention.

One journey in particular was the high point of the weekend. The intent was to see where a being goes after death. It began like all the others but then launched into one of the most beautifully profound journeys of my life. And it gave me an understanding I was longing for.

When the drumming started I restated my intent to discover where a being goes upon death, and was transported into the non-ordinary reality of walking down a snow-covered path. I felt—not heard—a deafening silence. The path was lined with enormous evergreens and I was cocooned in the comfort of their nurturing, age-old wisdom. Then a peace, intense and all-encompassing, lifted me, like being pulled by a strong but gentle magnet, into a void of nothingness, yet in the All. I was suffused with a sense of intense joy and freedom and although I was still aware of my physical body, a part of me was being lifted from it.

As I rounded a bend on the path, I was pulled, or almost yanked, as if by a powerful magnet and merged with a light of unbelievable brilliance. I *became* the brilliance. I *was* the light. The only way to define something so indefinable is that I was floating in a knowing. I *was* knowing. I simply . . . was. No longer aware of myself experiencing this journey, the "I" of me vanished into an abyss of pure experience—the infinity of all-knowing, all-loving.

When the quickened drumbeat pulled me back into this reality, tears began to flow. I didn't want to leave that paradise, and I cried from the pure ecstasy of the experience and from gratitude in realizing that this blissful state was inside *me*—had always been inside me—and that it is inside all beings and is what links us all as one.

~

As my body slowly regained wakefulness, I felt, to some degree, anesthetized. I lay motionless, wishing that the drunken ecstasy I still felt would infuse every cell of my being so that I could recall it at any time. Tears of joy and gratitude continued to slowly roll down my face. Then, much like waking from a dream, I began feeling fully present in my body. What only moments before had seemed so real in non-ordinary reality ebbed away into becoming simply a memory—albeit an extraordinary and unforgettable one.

In the moments while I still lay integrating this journey, I was relieved that I now had an idea where Charlie would go when he died. I no longer cared about the semantics of what or where Heaven, the Other Side, or the afterlife was. Maybe it was non-ordinary reality as defined by shamans, or the astral region as defined by Eastern philosophy. But whatever one might choose to call it, I had experienced this "place," and I knew it was there.

This new perception of death gave me a better understanding of life. I realized that in looking at the grand scale of the entirety of a being's existence, I could see both life and death as simply experiences of that being. Neither life nor death is more satisfying or superior than the other. From the standpoint of a physical life, the beauty of life after death may appear more appealing, but it is only a different, spiritual experience of that being. And anyone can tap into this higher awareness by placing his or her attention there through journeying or meditation.

∾

I was no longer afraid of death itself and even felt peaceful about what would happen to Charlie and where he would go when he died. Yet it was still difficult to detach myself from the impending sorrow of life without him. I wondered—would this newly found understanding of death be enough to get me through the heartache of losing him?

I did not yet know the spiritual significance of Charlie's cancer, but what I did know was that it was causing me to grow spiritually in spite of myself.

There was still a missing piece about death that I needed to understand. But the obstacle was that I didn't know what the missing piece was. I just knew the puzzle wasn't complete. How the heck could I get an answer when I didn't even know the question? My biggest fear was that Charlie might die before I fulfilled my quest. Once again, I prayed for the only thing I knew to pray for: acceptance.

All It Took Was a Healing Touch

Several weeks after the shamanic workshop, an energy healer who had worked on Charlie said, "Why don't you learn some energy healing techniques yourself so that you can help Charlie on a daily basis?"

"Could you teach me?" I asked.

"I could, but I think it would be better for you to take a workshop. That way you can learn more proficiency with various techniques to help ease any pain Charlie might have and to strengthen his immune system. It might help the vaccine work more effectively, too."

"What's the workshop?"

"It's called 'Healing Touch for Animals®,' taught by a woman named Carol Komitor. I think there's a workshop here in the Chicago area next weekend. You really should check it out."

I did. There was indeed a class scheduled. I signed up.

Once again I found myself driving over an hour to yet a different south Chicago suburb. This time, however, I battled ugly Friday afternoon traffic. My flawed directions caused me to make a wrong turn and I drove around in a circle for about thirty minutes. When I found myself stopped at the same red light for the third time with still no clue where to go, my frustration peaked. I pounded the steering wheel and let fly a litany of expletives. In the midst of this temper tantrum I had a semi-out-of-body experience, and suddenly felt detached from the situation, as though I were the observer of this raging lunatic in the car. In those seconds of detachment, clarity came and I recognized the churning in my gut. It was not merely frustration from being lost. It was a churning that I had experienced on two other occasions in my life.

The first time it had occurred was right before I met my spiritual mentor, Ishwar. The second time was the night before starting Penelope's animal communication classes. Both times I had a strong yearning to flee due to a subconscious knowing that my life was about to change profoundly. And, indeed, both times it did change—for the better. So I prayed for courage and decided to try to embrace what lay ahead.

With the fog now lifted from my head, I pulled over, called the facility where the meeting was to be held, and got directions. I had been only blocks away the entire time.

The dark wood-paneled library that was to be our classroom for the evening had a very studious and warm feeling. I was surprised at how relaxed I felt as I sat in the circle, looking at my thirty fellow classmates before the class began. And Carol Komitor's easy, soft nature helped put me at ease.

For our introductory night, Carol spoke about how healers working with people and animals work with the chakras and energy fields (which I prefer to call essence fields) of the body.

"Can someone tell us what the word 'chakra' means?" she asked.

"It means 'wheel' or 'wheel of light,'" a man toward the front of the room offered.

"Yes," Carol said. "It's a Sanskrit word that dates back to the second century. It is said that healers have worked with chakras since ancient times, so it's not a New Age phenomenon. The seven chakras are whirlpools of energy, or energy processing centers that are located along the spinal column—starting with the first chakra at the coccyx, the second in the lower abdomen, the third in the solar plexus, the fourth in the middle of the chest, the fifth in the throat area, the sixth in the middle of the forehead behind the eyes, and the seventh at the crown, or top of the head."

Carol paused and continued. "The purpose of these techniques is to keep the energy in the chakras and body flowing to allow healing. If the energy in the body gets stagnant, say, from an injury, illness, or emotional issue, then problems can develop at the cellular level. I'll teach you techniques to help maintain balance of the chakras because if one chakra is unbalanced, other chakras may then be thrown off balance, which, in turn can cause other imbalances in the body."

Carol pointed to woman raising her hand. "Yes?"

"Will you be giving us a more concrete explanation of how energy healing works so that we can explain its benefits to people not familiar with it?"

"Yes," she responded. "I'd be happy to and I'm glad you asked. As practitioners, you also need to understand what I'm about to explain and then you can pass on your knowledge. The body's physiological response to energy healing is like a domino effect. Energy healing allows endorphins to kick in. This creates a relaxation response in muscles, which then allows better circulation and increases the body's level of oxygen. This, in turn, promotes healing and also helps the body detoxify. All of this helps in alleviating pain and boosting the immune system, which aids in healing."

"Can this help with cancer?" a woman behind me asked. I turned to look at this person who had asked exactly what was in my own mind.

"Good questions!" said Carol. "Yes, it can. And I'll tell you how. Cancer is embryonic in nature and cancer cells have a lower vibration than those in the rest of the body. Because of this slowed down embryonic state, the body thinks it needs to feed the tumor with blood. Thus cancer grows. Energy healing helps to raise the vibration of a malignant cell to inhibit or hopefully stop its growth. By keeping the body's basic vibration level raised, healthy cells can grow."

I felt so hopeful! Maybe I really *could* help Charlie!

To start us off, Carol had us go around the circle and, with our hands, try to sense each other's essence fields, which usually extend about eight to twelve inches from the body. To me, it felt like an invisible pressure or "wall." I could tell when an area of a body was compromised by perceiving this essence as closer to the body, or warmer, cooler, or a static vibration in a certain area. If I perceived any one of these, for example, in someone's right shoulder, I would ask if they had a problem there. Inevitably the answer was yes. Although this was very similar to Reiki, another healing technique I had studied, what was new for me was that as I moved my hands, my palms felt tingly and alive—like they were "reading" or translating all on their own what was going on with a person. Sometimes my hands even felt as if they were being pulled or directed to an area that needed healing.

Then we practiced giving healing to others. Carol instructed us to feel the energy coming through a point in the palms of our hands to the other person. When I felt the healing flow through me, my palms pulsated warmth, like they were vibrating separately from the rest of my body. It felt like a current pulsing through my whole body and pouring out of my hands. The only way to describe this current was that it was like the compassion I'd felt from the whales, so I knew the origin of it to be the Divine.

The next day, the canine class was held in a large auditorium to accommodate everyone and their dogs. We spent the day learning various techniques and practicing our hands-on work with different dogs.

"Animals are easier to work with than people," Carol said. "The simple reason is that they don't have the complexity of our intellectual and emotional minds and they're more aware, energetically."

I already knew this, but now was literally getting hands-on proof. The dogs melted into the healing—even the ones who were a little hyper immediately calmed down.

Once again acting as Charlie's emissary, Toby came along as my hands-on guinea pig. Toby was delighted with all the attention he got and the healing he received. He was so relaxed by the end of the day that he instantly fell asleep when we got in the car and didn't wake up until we pulled into the garage over an hour later. When the car bumped over the garage threshold, Toby's sleepy face popped up, looked around, and then looked at me as if to say, "How the heck did we get *here?*"

The next day was Sunday—the day for working with horses. Originally I hadn't planned on taking this class. But during the night I awoke, realizing that I'd be cheating myself if I didn't. I was curious to know if the techniques would be different when applied to horses. Besides, it was a chance to be around horses again and, just maybe, I'd learn something else to help Charlie. So I went.

To demonstrate the extent of a horse's essence, Carol stood with a horse in the middle of the arena while we formed a large circle around them. She then asked us to step forward slowly until we could sense the essence field of the horse, either with our hands, our body, or our intuition. I took only six steps before my hands sensed the invisible barrier. No one needed to take more than twelve steps forward before they, too, could feel it and even then, they were still a good twenty feet from the horse. I was awestruck.

I then had a revelation about the whales. If the essence field of a thousand-pound horse extended twenty to thirty feet, then how far out would the essence of a seventy-ton whale extend? I now understood how I was able to feel the whales just by being in the water—even with no whale in sight. With hundreds of humpbacks in the Silver Bank, no wonder Penelope called it "whale soup"!

The work with the horses was profound—much more so than working with the dogs—and it grounded everything I had learned the day before. I worked with a horse who, not long before, had been rescued by this facility. After doing some healing on his old leg injuries, I connected with him heart to heart, using one of Carol's techniques working with the heart chakra. As I felt the essence of his heart expand and melted into it, I "saw" the kicks and whacks he had endured and "heard" the vile language that had been hurled at him by his former owners. The depth of sadness in his heart made me want to drop to my knees and weep. But the immense love and forgiveness in him bolstered me. In the moments of our heart exchange, I felt the compassion flowing through me fill his heart, and prayed this would help heal his sadness. And from him, from his quiet, rock-solid inner strength and dignity, I understood the exquisite gift of forgiveness.

I could have floated home that day. The workshop was over but my passion for healing was just beginning. I was elated to have found something that could help Charlie, maybe even heal him. And I was struck by the irony—Charlie's cancer had led me to my life's passion. What a price to pay. Yet what a gift.

~

Both Charlie and Toby loved the healing. Charlie got so accustomed to his treatments that when I gestured for him to get on the couch and said, "Come on, Baby Boy! Let's do some healing on you!" he'd jump up and flop down expectantly. Then less than a minute later, he'd be sound asleep. Because of his daily treatments, Charlie could walk further without tiring and was more energetic overall. This gave me hope and peace of mind that at least I was doing something to help him. Just maybe, I thought, since part of Charlie's purpose was to lead me to healing work, now he'd choose to stick around.

But in the back of my mind something kept nagging at me. I had heard and read stories about animals who, after fulfilling their purpose of leading their humans to their life's path, passed on.

~

The more experience I gained with healing, the more I realized how little I knew. But I was seeing that through whatever means—intuitive communication, shamanism, meditation, or energy healing—all are methods to access Spirit, inner wisdom, and Truth. And I grew to learn that it didn't really matter which method was used.

What I did know was that in doing the Healing Touch for Animals® chakra balance techniques, I was able to sense what to me felt like static, warmth, or coolness of the chakras when they were imbalanced. And when balanced, they felt like they were humming in tune—there was an effervescence about them. Then I began to wonder how the chakras worked. *What* made them work? If chakras are energy processing centers, what are they processing? And where does the energy come from that they process?

I went to the only person I knew who could give me answers—Ishwar.

"Well," he said. "Chakras are the means by which our physical, emotional, mental, and spiritual selves merge together." He paused.

I sat, eagerly waiting for him to continue.

"They are the six gateways through which our non-physical spiritual Self brings consciousness to the body *and* through which we are able to access higher awareness."

"Six? I always thought there were seven?"

"It depends on how you look at it," he said. "If you only consider the physical body, then you could say there are seven."

"So . . . what's the significance of whether or not there are six or seven chakras?"

"The significance," he said, his eyes beaming like he was about to divulge one of the best-kept secrets in the Universe, "is that when all the chakras of the physical, astral, and causal bodies overlap, they all link up in the heart chakra."

"So is this linking of the heart chakras, sort of like the main power cord, what actually makes us conscious beings?"

He nodded.

"So . . . if the chakras, specifically the heart chakra, as you say, make us conscious, living beings, then . . . they would have a role in the process of death—or in the moment of death. Right?"

He nodded again. "That's right."

"Then that's it!" I said, springing forward. "That's the missing piece about death I want to know!"

His eyes twinkled.

"I want to know how the shift of death happens!" I said excitedly. "Exactly how and at what point does the life force leave the body?" I implored.

He smiled affectionately. "I know how much you want to understand this. But it's too much to go over right now," he said, glancing at his watch. "And now I have to go. We can discuss this next time."

"No!" I begged and grabbed his arm like a six-year-old. "I've seen *where* Charlie's life force will go. But I want to be in tune with him every step of the way so I know what's happening with him. I need to know how the life force leaves!"

"And you will!" he said. He rose from his chair and gently rested his hand on my cheek. "You will. Just not today."

The compassion in his eyes melted my frustration. I knew he was speaking Truth. I knew the answer would come. I just had to be patient.

The Blinders Come Off

Weeks later, though it pained me to admit it, I noticed that Charlie was showing signs of slowing down. At first the daily healings had helped, but now he was getting fatigued on his walks. I feared the vaccine wasn't working or that he had made the decision to go. Either way, I couldn't bear to know the truth.

At the end of May I took Charlie to my regular vet, Dr. Pat, for another chest X-ray. The lung tumors had grown, but only slightly. I called Dr. Alexi at UW-Madison with these results.

"This could be a good sign," he said. "It could mean the vaccine is working by forming an arsenal of antibodies around the tumors to dissolve them."

"That's hopeful," I said.

"But we don't really know for sure. Let's hope for the best. As a reminder, the tumor in Charlie's mouth might begin to bleed—maybe even profusely. These tumors in the mouth can bleed easily, but with the tissue being cancerous, the tumor could bleed with no warning or provocation."

"We haven't had any episodes of bleeding so far, although I have noticed some small blood stains in areas where he lies his head."

"I don't think that's anything to worry about," Dr. Alexi said. "Keep me posted."

"I will. Thanks for the warning," I said.

As it turned out, I was very grateful for the warning.

On Memorial Day, Steve and I enjoyed the warm, sunny afternoon planting flowers in the front yard. Toby took a siesta on the couch while Charlie sat inside the front door doing his self-appointed sentry duty and watching every move Steve and I made. I dashed inside for a drink of water and noticed pools of blood on the floor around where Charlie had been sitting. Then I saw blood dripping from his mouth. Charlie didn't seem the least bit bothered and greeted me enthusiastically. I tried to settle him down so I could get a good look in his mouth. I parted his lips.

"Steeeve!" I screamed. "Get in here!"

Steve came barreling through the door. "What's the . . . " he said, looking at the blood on the floor and then at Charlie. "Is that from his mouth?"

"Yeah! His whole mouth is filled with blood!" I said, panicked.

"I'll grab some towels and an ice pack."

We got Charlie settled quietly on the couch under layers of old towels and held the ice pack to his cheek.

"Do you think this is what Dr. Alexi meant by bleeding profusely?" I asked.

"Let's hope it's the tumor that's bleeding," Steve said. "There's so much blood in his mouth it's hard to see where it's coming from."

Just then Charlie coughed and threw up a large pool of blood.

"We're going to the emergency vet," I said. "What if the blood is coming from his lungs?"

"Well, let's just hope it isn't," Steve said, picking him up.

I held Charlie on my lap in the back seat, and by the time we reached the emergency clinic, his mouth had stopped bleeding. By all appearances he was fine. "Charlie's lungs sound clear," the emergency vet told us. "They're not congested. I think it's safe to assume that the blood he threw up he ingested from the mouth tumor."

"But how can we be sure?" I asked.

"Unfortunately, other than doing an extremely invasive procedure to scope the lungs, there is no way to be sure."

"Well, I wouldn't put him through that," I said.

"I don't see a need for it, either," the vet said. "See how he does tonight and tomorrow and if there are any problems, call or bring him back in."

On the drive home I sat in the back with Charlie and watched him gaze attentively out the window.

"God, I can't stand the uncertainty of this," I said.

"It sucks," Steve said, "but his lungs are clear. So let's focus on that."

That evening, in case the tumor bled again, I rolled up all my rugs and covered the sofa and bed (the "dogs allowed" furniture) with layers of old blankets. While smoothing out an old green and blue comforter on top of the bed, a twisting ache in my gut told me the truth about Charlie. He was not going to get better. Tears spilled down my cheeks. I realized that despite all of my insights, I had been living in a childlike bubble, the one where we refuse to believe our parents, animals, or anyone close to us will ever *really* die.

As I sat on the edge of the bed staring zombie-like out the window, I knew it was time to face the hideous truth. Charlie would die sometime soon, probably from the cancer. Did I have the courage to face it?

I acknowledged that my self-focused "you can't leave me" attitude wasn't doing Charlie any good. I had always leaned on Charlie for emotional support. He knew my innermost heart in *all* its nakedness, knew of all my struggles in life and the deepest pains that I sometimes walled off even from myself. His love had always recharged me. Now it was time for me to grow up and stand on my own so that Charlie could lean on me.

I went downstairs to find my boys on the couch—Steve sitting in the middle with Charlie on one side and Toby on the other. "Three peas in a pod!" I said, and gave each a kiss.

"There's no other place I'd rather be," Steve said. "Sandwiched between my two best buddies."

"Well, is there room for me?" I asked.

"I guess if we have to we can make room for one more," Steve said laughing. "Here," he said moving over. "Sit between Charlie and me."

"I think I'm going crazy," I said, sitting down and hugging Charlie.

"How would you know?" Steve said with a chuckle.

"I mean it. I really feel sometimes like I'm losing it," I said, and gently rubbed Charlie's back. "I've had all of these profound insights about death, so you'd think I'd be somewhat at peace with this whole thing. But I just can't face losing him."

"I don't think anything or anyone can adequately prepare you for this," Steve said. "You can read about it and talk about it but you never know how you're going to deal with it until it happens. And Charlie has been the most important figure in your life for the past twelve years."

"I know. But I've been running all over the place trying to understand death and when it comes right down to it, I'm not so sure it has helped."

"I'd have to disagree with that," Steve said.

"Why?" I said, and wiped a tear from my cheek.

"Well, think about it for a minute. Wouldn't it be worse without the things you've learned? Wouldn't it be even harder?"

"Yeah, I guess."

"Without a doubt. I think your experiences have enabled you to stay in control and not give in to panic. And because you don't give in to panic, this has a calming effect on Charlie."

"But I *am* panicky!" I said.

"I disagree. It's not panic. It's fear. Fear of the unknown. The worst fear there is."

"I just can't imagine him not being here," I said, and buried my face in Charlie's fur.

∼

Though the tumor never bled badly again, in the weeks that followed there were always droplets of blood wherever Charlie lay down. We put an ice pack under his right jaw—the side of the tumor—to alleviate any soreness and inflammation. This soothed him. He also received regular acupuncture from the veterinarian, massage from a friend, and energy healing from me. From the way he gingerly ate his softened food, it was obvious that the tumor in his mouth was now causing him discomfort. Otherwise, he was still his attentive, playful, sometimes feisty, and loving self.

Over the next couple of weeks, the oral tumor began rapidly increasing in size. His right cheek became noticeably protruded. I called Dr. Alexi.

"Unfortunately," he said, "there is really no way of knowing whether the tumor itself has grown—which would mean the cancer has spread—or if the vaccine has built immune bodies around it, which could also cause it to increase in size."

When Charlie began having trouble eating and swallowing, I took him to the specialty clinic. The vet could see that the tumor was growing on the inside, way in the back of his mouth. He recommended surgery. I agreed. I checked in with Charlie to make sure he was okay with this. He was willing, he said, to undergo one surgery, but was very clear that he wanted no further invasive treatments.

Spiritual Guidance

A few days later I took Charlie to the specialty clinic for surgery to remove the tumor. Before leaving for the clinic, I held him on the couch and explained and visualized what he would go through that day. I really had to focus on sticking with the facts and not get my emotions into it. I was relieved to discover how keeping my emotions out of it helped *me* stay positive.

"As soon as we finish the surgery I'll call you on your cell phone to let you know what we find," the surgeon said. "He should be ready to go home sometime late this afternoon."

"I'm worried about post-surgery pain and how he'll be able to eat. Will you prescribe anything for pain?"

"Yes. We'll give him something for pain. And we'll give you enough liquid food to last a few days."

I gave Charlie a kiss on the nose before he willingly trotted out of the room with the surgeon.

Not wanting to spend the entire day at home fretting over Charlie, I took my car to the dealership for a scheduled servicing. I sat in the waiting room for a while and got antsy while waiting for my friend, Doris, to come pick me up for lunch. I went outside and meandered down the rows of new cars. I was mindlessly staring at a car sticker price when the shrillness of my cell phone startled me.

My heart knocked against my chest as I frantically rummaged in my purse to grab my phone.

"Ms. Bumbera?"

Adrenaline shot through me when I recognized the surgeon's voice.

"Yes," I answered nervously.

"Charlie is doing very well," he said in a humdrum tone. "He made a very quick recovery from the anesthesia. The tumor that we removed from the back of his mouth and throat was about the size of a golf ball."

I was speechless. No wonder Charlie had trouble eating. My mind wandered for a few seconds, feeling horrible for him, and I didn't quite catch what the surgeon was saying—something about cancer and the jawbone.

"Well, how will we know if it has spread to the jawbone?" I asked.

In an incredulous tone, smacking of "Didn't you hear me the first time?" he said, "I *know* it's in the jawbone."

Without giving me a chance to digest this, much less respond, he said, "Charlie will be ready to go home at about four o'clock. The only treatment we can do for him is radiation to inhibit further growth. I'll be happy to discuss this with you when you come to pick him up today."

We said goodbye. Robotically, I placed my cell phone in my purse and slowly zipped it shut. I struggled to comprehend what I had just heard. The sea of cars around me along with the cacophony of traffic on the nearby street seemed surreal—like a scene from a movie I was watching instead of a part of my own reality. An angelic presence must have intervened, reminding me to breathe. Then it hit. Bone cancer! I wasn't naïve enough to think the vaccine could put that in remission. And the surgeon's lack of compassion had left me feeling as if I had been sliced open and left to bleed.

I was relieved to see Doris' car pull up. As I got in, she asked cheerily, "Where do you want to go for lunch?"

I shrugged. I had done my best not to break down and cry in the car lot and now I was in the comfort of a good friend. But the aching constriction in my throat made it impossible to utter a word.

I avoided eye contact, foolishly thinking she wouldn't notice something was wrong. But being the sensitive, caring friend she is, my silence and actions spoke loudly.

"Did you talk to the surgeon?" she asked tentatively.

I stared straight ahead, but couldn't meet her gaze. Tears began tumbling down my cheeks.

"Do you want me to just drive?"

I nodded.

When I finally was able to talk, Doris, whose two cats had recently died, cried with me. Why we didn't pull over I don't know, but there we were, two women driving down the thoroughfare of a northern Chicago suburb, crying.

We stopped for a lunch of comfort food—veggie burgers, French fries, and chocolate shakes at a pleasant outdoor café. Fortified by the meal, I now felt strong enough to make the call I was dreading—to tell Steve of the bone cancer diagnosis. Steve was in Ohio because just one week earlier, his father, who he loved and utterly adored, had died. Over the course of the week, Steve had mentioned how grateful he was that he had me, Charlie, and Toby to help him through his grief. And now I had to tell him that he would soon be facing another loss.

Steve took the news hard. "I've only had two heroes in my life," he said. "My dad and Charlie. Soon they'll both be gone." In the fourteen years I had known Steve,

I had never heard such pain in his voice. And there was nothing I could say or do to comfort him.

When I went to pick Charlie up, the surgeon was very accommodating. He took his time explaining the surgery and what the treatment options were.

"The only option for the bone cancer is weekly radiation," he said. "The radiation itself is not invasive. But the danger is that the radiation could hit the eye instead of the jaw if Charlie moves even slightly during the procedure. To avoid this risk, he would need to be anesthetized for each radiation treatment."

"That seems too much to put him through," I said, remembering that Charlie had told me he didn't want any further invasive treatment. "Is there any guarantee that the radiation would substantially increase his quality of life?"

"We can't guarantee anything. But unfortunately, your only other option is to do nothing."

"Well, the options aren't good," I said. "I don't think we'll do any further treatment, but if we do, I'll certainly be in touch."

Then a vet tech brought Charlie in the room. He made a beeline to me, wagging his tail. "You look great!" I said to him and gave him a hug. He went and stood by the door as if to say, "Yeah, yeah. C'mon! Can we get outta here?"

"He doesn't even look like he's had surgery," I said with relief.

"Call if you have any questions or concerns," the surgeon said. "The vet tech will go over the pain patch with you. Good luck," he said, and walked out the door.

"You probably noticed the patch on Charlie's right front leg," said the technician.

"Yeah, I did. I thought it was a bandage."

"That's a Fentanyl pain patch. It will take six hours to be fully effective. Because Fentanyl is a controlled substance—meaning it's a narcotic—it can only be removed by veterinary personnel. So you can take Charlie to your vet to have it removed. You don't need to bring him back here."

"Okay," I said. "I'm just glad he's got some pain relief."

"And here is his food," she said, handing me a bag. "There are instructions inside, but you just mix it with water. There are also a couple syringes in there to feed him with because he won't be able to chew anything for a few days."

That evening Charlie was in great spirits. I syringed the food to my hungry boy. But by midnight, his breathing had become labored and he couldn't sit or lie still. Then he started yelping. Panicked, I called the clinic where he had had the surgery.

"You need to bring him in," said the emergency veterinarian.

The clinic was busy and during our hour-long wait, Charlie became even more agitated, panting heavily and yelping more frequently. By this time, I was so stressed I wanted to yelp, too. I tried some healing techniques and sang to him—but nothing would calm him.

Finally the emergency vet came in. "Hello," he said to me without so much as a glance at Charlie. He read Charlie's medical records and seemed oblivious to Charlie's yelps. Then in a cold, terse manner, he said, "You know he's terminal."

His lack of compassion astonished me. Strangely enough, this word, *terminal*, that now reverberated in my head like echoes in a canyon, had never been used by any other veterinary personnel when describing Charlie's condition. And from this vet, the word seemed especially cruel.

He hurriedly examined Charlie.

"His heart is fine," he said in a clipped tone.

"He's been yelping like this for almost two hours," I said. "Could he be in pain?"

"No. There has been adequate time for the Fentanyl patch to take effect." Then he looked in Charlie's mouth again. "His teeth are very bad and his breath is putrid," he said. His eyes bored into me like it was my fault.

But I was too exhausted to do verbal battle with this veterinarian, who should have known that one indication of a cancerous oral tumor is putrid breath. I was too tired to bother to tell him that for the past month the tumor had oozed frequently and Charlie could no longer drink water on his own. Of course his teeth were bad.

"So what about the labored breathing and yelping?" I asked, exasperated.

"The cancer must have gone to his brain," he said matter of factly.

"In the past seven hours?" I asked.

He didn't respond. But then said, "It's not very likely, but it's a slight possibility that the Fentanyl patch is causing the distress. I can remove the patch, since it must be handled by veterinary personnel, or you can wait until morning to see how he's doing." Then without another word, he left the room.

I waited, thinking Dr. No-Heart would return. But thirty minutes later, when the door opened, a technician poked her head in.

"The doctor needs to know what you've decided," she said.

"I guess we'll just wait," I said snappishly, realizing I would get no further advice.

I paid the bill (for what, I didn't know) and left. It was now past two o'clock in the morning and Charlie was still yelping in distress. Since medical guidance was unobtainable, I prayed for the spiritual kind.

Once home, I again tried to calm Charlie down, but it was no use. By this time I needed calming just as much as he did.

"Okay!" I shouted to the Heavens. "I give up! I'm on my knees! Give me some guidance here! NOW!"

Within minutes, I knew intuitively, without a shred of doubt, that the Fentanyl patch was causing Charlie's distress. Deciding that veterinary personnel could kiss my derrière, I removed the patch. About an hour later Charlie stopped yelping and finally went to sleep. I got in bed and wedged myself between Charlie and Toby and nuzzled my face into the soft curls of Charlie's neck as we both drifted off into dreamland.

The next day Charlie was a bit woozy, but quickly returned to his normal self.

Later that morning I learned from Dr. Alexi and Dr. Pat that Charlie's reaction to Fentanyl wasn't typical but also was not uncommon. Couldn't someone have warned me?

Dream a Little Dream . . .

A few days later I tuned in to Charlie while snuggling him one afternoon to see if he wanted radiation treatments—just in case. I conveyed the procedure to him, telling him verbally and visually, step by step, to the best of my ability. He said no, he didn't want to go through that. I asked about the vaccine and healings—he was fine with receiving them, he said. While tuned in to him, I sensed an overall fatigue and slowing down in his body that I hadn't felt before. This bothered me, but since he still had one last vaccine scheduled, I clung to the shred of hope that it might revive him—or at least buy him a little more time.

In the beginning of July, Charlie received his last vaccine. (And although each dose of the vaccine took one hour of prep time before administering, Dr. Pat never charged me a dime. A true testament that generous, kind-hearted people really do exist!) Though Charlie was still enjoying his walks and rides in the car, his stride continued to slow and the tired look in his eyes showed that he didn't feel well. Days later, I came to the realization that my job as caretaker had changed. I was no longer needed to help Charlie live, but to help him die.

I called Dr. Alexi.

"Well, I'm sorry," he said. "From everything you've said, it appears the vaccine didn't work. By now we would've seen some kind of improvement. At least you have some peace in knowing you did all you could for him."

"Thank you for all you've done," I said.

I lived with a constant panic about discovering how the shift of death takes place. I wanted to understand it before Charlie died so that I could be more aware of what he was experiencing—be with him every step of the way, so to speak—and hoped that the understanding would help ease my grief. Intuitively I knew the answer would come. But how? And *when?* Ironically, I believe it was my surrender to the truth that Charlie was dying that had opened the door to the elusive answer.

It came one early morning of July in a dream. Though I often received insights and messages in dreams, it hadn't occurred to me that I would receive the answer this way—it was sort of like watching a 3D video with the information being downloaded into me. I dove for pen and paper and frantically wrote before the insight faded. It was this:

Each chakra in the physical body has its own resonance, like a series of vibrations or tones or music, and when they combine all together, much like instruments in an orchestra, along with the resonances of the astral and causal chakras, a single unique mega-resonance of that being is created. This mega-resonance is the life force that sustains consciousness in that being.

An illness or injury causes a dissonance of a chakra or chakras (like a few instruments in an orchestra playing out of tune or out of rhythm) and, over time, the mega-resonance or life force itself is affected by the untuned "players." It becomes untuned itself and slows to the point that it can no longer sustain itself in the physical body. So when the physical chakras "stop playing" and can no longer sustain themselves in the body, the astral and causal chakras begin pulling away from the physical—beginning with the lower chakras first. Yet even though the astral and causal chakras pull away from the physical chakras, the link at the heart center can still remain intact for quite a while. However, the instant this link splits or breaks off, death occurs. The essence, or unique resonance, of the being simply leaves the physical body, but is carried on in the astral and causal bodies. The astral and causal bodies survive on their own and remain the same.

As I lay back down, assimilating this, I thought about dying people who said they couldn't feel their feet or legs. Now this made sense to me.

This insight—this final piece of the puzzle—gave me a clearer understanding that death really does only pertain to the physical body. And that the essence, or Spirit, of a being does indeed live on.

Filled with gratitude, I looked over at Charlie, who was still sleeping soundly. I watched him for a few moments, then gently rubbed the top of his head, leaned down to him, and softly sang his morning song. "Wake up, wake up you sleepyhead. Get up, get up, get outta bed."

He opened his eyes and stretched out his hind legs.

"C'mon, Baby Boy. Wanna go outside?"

I watched him sleepily sit up and felt a deep peace knowing that "he" wouldn't die—and that the love I felt from and for him would never die.

But an instant later the gnawing anguish of losing him seized me once again.

Never in my life had I ridden such an emotional roller coaster.

At least the crest of emotion soon to come would provide clarity.

More Healing Gifts

My birthday, around this same time, was bittersweet. I wanted to celebrate that Charlie was still with me. Yet I knew it would be the last birthday I would be sharing with him.

Charlie's condition continued to deteriorate and caring for him was becoming physically taxing. It was still too difficult for him to chew, so I had to syringe-feed him liquid food that I pureed in the food processor four times a day. I was also constantly washing the towels I kept under his mouth because the original site of the tumor above the gum line was oozing foul-smelling bloody liquid. I had to get up with him once or twice each night when he needed to go outside or if he was restless and needed comforting. By this time he was also having bouts of diarrhea that needed to be cleaned up if I couldn't get him outside fast enough. Though I treasured this time taking care of him, I wondered if this was any way for either of us to live.

Despite his physical weakening, whenever I asked, "Do you want to go for walkies?" his tail would wag with excitement and he would enjoy every step of his walk, sniffing and lifting his leg in each desirable spot. Every evening I took both boys for a ride in the car—Toby, of course, riding shotgun in front while Charlie sat regally in the back, observing the passing scenery as though it was all part of his beloved kingdom.

I felt at peace in intuitively knowing that Charlie wasn't ready to go yet. So why, I kept asking myself, was I beside myself with grief when Charlie hadn't even died yet? I knew he wouldn't be lost to me forever. I understood from him that he would someday return to me. There had to be an emotional component I had not yet unearthed.

With the stress causing much tension in my body, I made an appointment with a massage therapist/healer. I had never met Carmela before but her training in integrating both emotional and spiritual awareness intrigued me.

As she led me to the massage room, I said, "Just so you know, my body is probably a mess because I'm under exceptional stress. My dog is dying."

"Oh, I'm really sorry," she said tenderly.

"I feel like I'm going nuts because I've attained a peaceful understanding of death, but I'm absolutely distraught by the reality of losing him. And this see-saw of emotion is making me absolutely crazy."

"Let's sit down," Carmela said, gesturing for me to sit in a cozy-looking overstuffed chair. "Is it okay if we talk for a minute first?"

"Yeah," I shrugged. "I guess."

She looked at me curiously and said, "Have you ever felt this same pain in your life before?"

My temper flared. I wanted to say, "What the hell kind of question is *that?*" But she had such compassion in her eyes and after all, wasn't I there to get some help?

"Maybe," I said a little defensively.

"Do you want to take a moment?" she asked. "Maybe close your eyes and feel it out?"

I let out a big sigh. "Yeah. I guess I should."

I took a few big, deep, slow breaths to calm myself and then took an account of my life, searching for an emotional match to what I was feeling.

"Yeah," I winced. "I have felt all of this before."

"Well, you don't have to tell me," she said. "Just as long as you know."

The relaxation of the massage helped me to open up the long-sequestered trauma of my parents' divorce.

At four years old I had been clueless about any marital problems between my parents. One night, which I still remember vividly, my dad solemnly told my older brother and me that, "Your mom doesn't think I love her anymore," and that he was no longer going to live with us. I couldn't understand. All I knew was that the person who tucked me in at night, fixed my breakfast, and comforted me when I had a nightmare was leaving.

Before this night, my brother and I had always played a game with Dad when he left the house. We would sit at the top of the staircase and wave continuously as he descended, yelling to him, "Bye, Dad! Bye!" Every few steps Dad would look up and wave back, say something funny, or blow us a kiss. But this night was different. As Dad descended the stairs my brother sat beside me crying while I waved and waved and waved at my dad, yelling the familiar, "Bye, Dad! Bye!" But my dad never even looked up. With his head down, he carried his suitcase down the stairs and was gone.

Through my adult eyes I can only imagine the heartbreak my dad felt at that moment. And I understand his inability to play our usual game. However, the four-year-old in me still carried this trauma of loss. Before he left, Dad had been our primary caretaker while my mother finished college. He had been the one to give me emotional support. Even though we saw him regularly after he moved out, my world never felt quite safe again. Until Charlie came into my life.

Now, facing Charlie's death, my four-year-old self's gaping wound of abandonment had resurfaced, wondering, "Who will take care of me? How will I be safe in the world? How will I survive without you? What is my place in the world without you? Who *am* I without you?"

And now, finally, I could see how and why I had grown up to be such a fearful adult. And why I had built a fortress around my heart. And why I had been so driven to keep myself safe and secure. *Finally* I could hold myself in compassion.

It was obvious that one purpose of having Charlie in my life was to heal this deep childhood trauma. I was now able to acknowledge how much emotional strength Charlie had given me during his twelve years. I realized that I was no longer that vulnerable, exposed, abandoned four-year-old that I sometimes felt I was. I realized that because of Charlie, I *did* feel safe enough to stand on my own in the world—to take my place in the world. And as a result of my quest of understanding death, I realized that I had gained a wealth of spiritual wisdom that could guide, support, and comfort me. Ironically, Charlie had given me what I needed so that I could cope with life without him.

That night as I snuggled him, nestling my face into his soft fur, I cried not because he was dying, but out of immense gratitude for the beautiful gifts he continued to give me.

Do We Have Free Will?

Still nagging at me was this question as to whether or not Charlie had, on some spiritual level, control over his cancer or a choice about dying or when he would die. Philosophers and mystics have long debated the issue of free will, so I didn't expect to find an answer, but I wanted a perspective my mind could accept.

As Ishwar and I settled into a corner table at a local café, I said, "I need to ask you about free will."

"Good!" he said with the ever-present sparkle in his eye that spoke of his joy of discussing spirituality. "What about it?" he asked, blowing on his tea to cool it.

"Well, I believe we have it. But I also know that there is a 'higher' spiritual wisdom to us all that we don't acknowledge or tap into."

"This is true," he said.

"So do we really have free will or does it just seem like we do because our attention and focus is 99 percent in this physical reality?"

"Did you just have a choice whether to buy coffee or tea?"

"Yeah. But I hemmed and hawed between a café mocha and a latte."

"But you made a choice. Isn't that free will?"

"Yeah. But that's coffee. What if I leave here and on the way to my car, I fall and break my leg. Did I choose that, too?"

"In your spiritual experiences you've shared with me," he said, "you said you experienced many different levels of consciousness, right?"

"Yeah, well, some I didn't experience thoroughly, but I experienced them. Are you suggesting that there are different levels of free will?"

"Yes," he said, taking a sip of tea. "It's what my teacher called 'human' free will and 'real' free will."

"What's the difference?" I leaned forward to hang on his every word.

"We have choices in every aspect of our lives—what we eat, the relationships we have, the clothes we wear, the career we choose, the house or car we buy, and what we attract in to our lives. We choose all things out of free will and feel that we are in control of our lives. This is 'human' free will."

"Got it," I said.

"But," Ishwar continued, "'human' free will does not give us a choice of who our parents are or of any unforeseen things that happen—such as accidents or cancer. So we realize we're not in control. And as you mentioned, this makes us ponder what free will we truly have. So it's like Shakespeare said—we are merely actors on a stage playing assigned roles without knowledge we are acting. Therefore, 'human' free will is a perceived free will."

"Perceived?" I asked. "You mean we don't really have it?"

"We *do* have it. Absolutely! But it depends on what level of consciousness you're considering."

"But in this physical level of consciousness," I said, "where we are, right here and now, we have free will. I can decide between a latte or mocha and choose to come here to meet you."

"Correct," he said. "'Human' free will."

"Then what is 'real' free will?"

"'Real' free will is from the highest level of consciousness. Let's call it Totality."

"Totality is the same as God, right?" I asked.

"Yes. God is Totality and Totality is God. This level of Totality—a timeless, space-less state—is total, or *is* Totality, because it comprises every single being in creation—human, animal, and plant. At this level, there is knowledge of the whole plan of creation. Also at this level, the experience of one being is chosen to experience one viewpoint of the Total. And this one viewpoint of the Total, meaning one being's life, is mapped out with predetermination of every minute detail. This is 'real' free will."

"Okay," I said and took a sip of coffee to fortify myself. "Let me make sure I understand. 'Real' free will originates from the level of Totality. Totality chooses one being in which to experience one viewpoint—and that viewpoint is completely predetermined. But when that viewpoint of Totality lives its life in the physical reality, it then has 'human' free will. So, really, we possess both 'human' *and* 'real' free will because we are multidimensional beings. Only we're not aware of our 'real' free will. Is this right?"

"Yes! You're right!" Ishwar said with a big smile.

"Wow!" I said and threw my hands up. "I just had a huge paradigm shift of thought—that 'I' with all my insecurities, neuroses, and gifts am a viewpoint of God, of Totality! And that—"

"Don't you see," Ishwar interrupted. "It means you *are* God. You *are* Totality just as *ALL* living things are! Your life is merely a viewpoint, or an individuation, of Totality!"

"Wow!" I paused to try and take this in. "This gives me a whole new understanding of Oneness and that all beings are connected." I paused again. "So . . . we really are actors, or like marionettes on a stage—just as Shakespeare said. So what, then, is the point of all this?"

"Have you ever heard it said that loneliness is the reason for Genesis? That God as Totality wants to experience him or her self?" he asked.

"Yes, I've heard that."

"'Human' free will is a blessing," he said. "Because we experience choices. If we had knowledge of our 'real' free will, or our destiny, we'd be like robots. And then we wouldn't learn or grow from our experiences. And humans, with their intellect, are the only beings capable of seeking God. So Totality, or God, blesses us with 'human' free will so that eventually, we can find our way back to our God-self, which is our true self."

"And," I said, "through both 'human' and 'real' free will, Totality can experience every infinitesimal aspect of itself. So spiritually speaking, wouldn't this mean that when bad things happen, it is Totality experiencing the wholeness of itself? Because wholeness of Totality must include duality—good *and* bad things, right?"

"That's right," Ishwar said.

"But . . . wait . . . I can understand why Totality might choose to experience the viewpoint of Charlie, an animal friend who is cherished and adored. But why would Totality choose the viewpoint or destiny of a person or animal who suffers unspeakable abuse or the ravages of war?" I asked.

"This depends on your definition of destiny," Ishwar said. "If you define destiny as only pertaining to one particular physical life, then unfortunate things, indeed, are experienced as unfair and tragic. But if you look at destiny from the perspective of Totality, then destiny is the conglomeration of *all* the lifetimes one being can have."

"Okay. Let me get this straight," I said. "So an analogy would be like thinking that one tiny grain of sand on a beach represents my destiny, which for this lifetime, it would. But from the aspect of Totality, my destiny is the infinite grains of sand on an endless beach?"

"Correct."

"Okay," I said, heaving a big sigh. "This fries my brain. I know this is the very tip, tip top of the iceberg in understanding this, but at least now I have a better perspective. This all started, you know, because of Charlie, so I want to be clear on how this ties in to him. Let me give a shot at what I understand."

"I'm ready," Ishwar said, crossing his legs and sitting back in his chair.

"Wait!" I said. "First I need clarity on how this translates to animals. From my experiences with animal communication and shamanic journeys, there is no spiritual difference between animals and people. So, I'm assuming that the 'real' and 'human' free will also applies to animals, is this right?"

"Yes, with one exception."

"Why does there *always* have to be an exception?" I said, heaving a big sigh. We both laughed. "Okay, what is it?"

"Animals do not have an intellect," he said. "Therefore they do not wrestle with ideas in the way that people do. So from an animal's perspective, they don't think they have free will. They are led by instinct. But spiritually speaking, the process of free will is basically the same."

"Basically?" I asked.

"Animals have an instinctual free will, meaning their free will is spontaneous, whereas humans have intellectual free will that is preceded by deliberation and thought."

"Okay. That makes sense," I said.

"So what clarity do you want about Charlie?" he asked.

"As of right now, this is what I understand about Charlie and me," I said. "Our lives were destined, or pre-destined, and it was already predetermined that Charlie would get cancer. How and when he will die has also been determined. And, through my 'human' free will, I have chosen to study animal communication, shaman-ism, and energy healing try to understand what death is and take care of Charlie in the way I have chosen to. But in truth, in the big picture of Totality, all of this has been predetermined. Am I right so far?"

"So far. Go on."

"But on some level, is it possible that Charlie is *in control* of his cancer? Can any being be in control of an illness?" I asked.

"No. No one can be in control of such a thing. *However,* from the 'human' free will perspective, a per-son can choose treatment and therefore feel in control of an illness. But you're right in saying that *ultimately,* from the perspective of Totality, everything has already been determined."

"This is so mind-bending," I said. "So all I know to do is revel in my 'human' free will and have faith that all will be taken care of regarding Charlie and me. *AND* listen to the wisdom inside me for guidance."

"AH! That's what I was waiting to hear!" Ishwar said, and threw his hand up. "Yes! Listen to the wisdom inside you! If you do that, you can never go wrong."

"Okay. I'll try. This gives me some peace in knowing that, as you say, all I can do is do my best and leave the rest."

"And remember," he said, "you yourself have experienced that when Charlie leaves his body, he will continue to live on. And you'll be able to connect with him. Don't forget that."

"Thank you." My eyes welled with tears. "Thank you for the reminder. It's still hard to say goodbye."

"You'll be okay. Don't worry," he said. "I'll help you. Charlie will help you." He stood up, bent down, and kissed my forehead. "You are well taken care of."

Seclusion

A few weeks after Charlie's surgery, the tumor on his gum began growing back very quickly. I willingly became a recluse to take care of him. With Steve in Ohio taking care of his mom and his father's estate, all I wanted was to be with Charlie and Toby. Except for occasional quick trips, I didn't leave the house. If friends hadn't brought me food, I probably would have lived on cereal, peanut butter toast, and popcorn. Whenever I returned home from my short outings, without fail, Charlie would be at the window or door waiting for me like he had done his whole life.

During this quiet time I did several shamanic journeys. I wanted information that would provide additional strength to deal with Charlie's death. The information I received was that Charlie and I, on some level, were one—that he was an extension or projection of me. I understood that Charlie had, in a sense, "split off" from me on some spiritual level. He appeared to me in my life as an aspect of myself, in a dog body, in order to bring me back to my true spiritual Self. In his passing, he would be a beacon of light assisting me in my spiritual growth and work even more intensely to awaken me. I understood that, in some way, I would be more whole after Charlie was gone because the part of me that was him would be working from a higher Spirit realm. And I understood that helping me in this way was one reason Charlie was leaving at this time, since this work could only be done from the Spirit realm.

This helped ease my heart. From this journey I understood that soulmates can be in animal form.

~

"Despite everything, I still keep expecting to be more at peace with Charlie's death," I said to Steve on the phone one night. "And on top of all this I'm sorry we can't be there with you. I feel I'm not supporting you because I'm so enmeshed in my own pain."

"I wish *I* could be there with *you*," he said with great sadness in his voice. "The timing of this couldn't be worse. Losing a parent—well, you can't know what it's like until it happens. Lucky for me, the insights you've had have helped me with losing my dad. But you know as well as I do—you gotta go through the process. And grieving is a part of it—spiritual knowledge or not."

"I just thought that if I had the answers, it would be easier," I said.

"The deeper you love, the harder you grieve," said Steve.

"So I guess it's like the Mayan belief—grief is a way of showing honor, respect, and love. But if I'm in this much pain now, what's it going to be like when he's gone?"

"One day at a time," Steve said. "Today he's still here."

Toby was also having a difficult time with Charlie's impending death. My exceptionally gentle, mild-mannered, dog-friendly Toby was suddenly barking aggressively at other dogs on our walks. Fortunately, this behavior was only temporary. To ensure objectivity, I called Carol Schultz to do a session with him.

"He says he doesn't mean to act out—his aggression is like a steam-valve," Carol said. "He's releasing his sadness that Charlie is dying. He said that when you cry, you help him work through his sadness."

"What else can I do to help him?" I asked.

"He says he wants longer walks and more healing to assist him with the grief."

"I can do that. I worry that my stress is taking a toll on him. Does it affect him?"

"It affects him like it would any family member. He's okay. He's very sad, but he's okay."

"Does he mind that Charlie gets almost all of my attention?"

"No. Not at all. He loves Charlie and he knows how much you love Charlie. He's okay with being in the background."

It always warmed my heart to see Toby asleep next to Charlie or cuddled up close to him. I could feel that Toby did this partly to protect Charlie, but I also felt Toby shared my urgency in getting as much physical "Charlie" comfort as he could. Of course this provided much comfort to Charlie as well.

I began getting increasingly anxious about Charlie's final moments. I knew it wouldn't be long and I feared my emotional pain wouldn't allow me to recognize when he was ready to go. Although I knew I would have to do whatever was best for Charlie, I prayed he would slip out of his body on his own. I wasn't sure I was courageous enough for the euthanasia process, though again I knew that was selfish. If we did have to go the euthanasia route, I prayed for the strength to hold and sing to him.

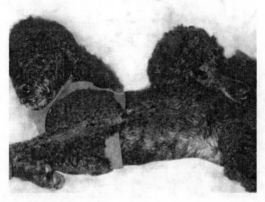

Toby using Charlie as a pillow

Soon Charlie became so lethargic and ill-looking, despite the twice-weekly acupuncture, large daily doses of baby aspirin, and my healing, that it was obvious these treatments no longer buffered his pain. Dr. Pat prescribed a potent anti-inflammatory and pain reliever. This perked him up enough so that he could once again enjoy his walks and car rides.

One afternoon I was helping Charlie lie down when he gave me a look that said it all. He was tired of living like this. He was tired of needing assistance and loathed the disfiguring golf-ball-sized tumor on the right side of his face. It was difficult to bear for one as proud and dignified as he. The tumor was obviously bigger on the inside because his right eye was beginning to bulge out slightly. I could tell he was almost blind in that eye.

Regardless, he was very peaceful about his impending death. When I tuned in to him, he said he was only

Charlie sleeping on Toby

worried for me. I repeatedly told him that although it was difficult for me, I wanted him to go whenever he needed to. I didn't want him to hang on for me, as I knew some animals did for their people. In a far corner of my mind was the thought that it was all predetermined anyway, so why should I worry? But philosophical concepts were not much comfort now.

I feared my grief was preventing me from accurately interpreting what was going on with Charlie, so I called my friend and fellow animal communicator, Kat Berard.

"These are the questions I need answers to," I said. "Is his pain tolerable? Is he ready to leave his body? If not, is he getting close to doing so? How will I know when he is ready?"

"Okay," she said. "I'll do the session tonight. I'll write out the transcript and email it to you. Is it okay if I ask him other questions that come up?"

"Yes, of course."

This is most of what came from the session. The pill or medicine referred to is the potent anti-inflammatory and the pain reliever he was taking.

How are you feeling this evening, Charlie?

A bit peppier, thank you [said solemnly, as if nodding].

I'm so glad to hear that! Does the medicine that Mary Ann gave you help you? Is that why you're feeling a bit better?

Yes, definitely. It takes the edge off, so my constant attention is not focused on how to ride this one out.

And that sounds peaceful for you.

Yes. At the moment. Later, when this feeling comes back, it won't be such a wonderful place to be. I grit my teeth and rock and roll with the feeling, the waves, as best I can. It smoothes out, then comes again. The work that Mary Ann and others do and have done with me is helpful, I appreciate the loving way they address me, but I continue to rock and roll [meaning he gets unbalanced in his energy].

That's lovely, Charlie. I'm so glad you've been able to receive this loving kindness from them. Mary Ann would like to know if your pain is bearable still, or is it becoming too much?

Too much. Too much. But then again, the medicine is freeing, lightening, it is cooling. My body feels cooler to me. Not pulsing as it has been.

What about the energy work Mary Ann and others do with you—would you like that continued? Is it helpful?

Yes, as I mentioned already. [He is to make sure I'm paying attention; he doesn't like to repeat himself.] *It is very soothing, it does give me relief, but it is short-lived. Perhaps*

*a few hours or through the night. So she and they may keep
doing this, but there will come a point where my body no longer accepts it.*

**Okay. Do you want assistance with your transition to
the Other Side?**

I'm not sure. In what manner?

**Such as that healing work, or Spirit helpers assisting
you—which I'm assuming yours will, but Mary Ann
may call on others as well to be with you—or medical
intervention such as a shot that helps you relax and
then another that would let your Spirit free itself from
your body.**

*I see. Well . . . [He ponders for a while.] I would like my
departure to be smooth, as I am feeling now. I do not want
to suffer through the indignity of losing control of my body.
[He is very clear that he doesn't want to go through the
death throes.] I like the feeling this medicine gives me, and
I would like this same type of feeling as I leave. If not, and the
way you mention [meaning euthanasia] is the way to do this
peacefully, then that would be okay as well. But truly, I would
prefer to pass peacefully, in my beloved's arms.*

**That feels like such a beautiful way to leave here,
Charlie. To have those you love around you. And your
guardian angels and other benevolent beings with and
around and waiting for you. I sense you will leave with
no physical pain left to hold you to your body.**

*No. I will just take a breath, and float and then fly away. I will
be All Light, All Love, All One with that and them [meaning
the Universe and his beloved companions—Mary Ann,*

Toby, Steve, animal playmates, human friends, vet personnel who have assisted him, healers and communicators, all those who have helped him in this journey to Home]. *There is no more pain, you just melt into the Light. It is breathtaking—literally—and breathgiving. It takes away, flows through, gives back. And there is no separation, just a shift.*

As you are leaving, is there anything you'd like Mary Ann to do, besides hold you?

She has such a lovely, soothing voice. If she would sing or hum to me, or just speak softly to me—I know her pain is great, and it is okay with me if she wishes to speak to me of that and let it flow through me and out into the Universe. It will come back as my loving energy. She will know this. I do not want her to worry she is not doing enough at that time. I want her to be okay with just being in the moment, with the moment, and feeling the purity of the shift.

We are of One, she and I. We have had many moments of clarity and knowingness, of unspoken connections that transcend words or feelings. She is of such Light and harmony and love [with this I heard/sensed angels singing or vibrating]; we are of that same energy. We have taken many steps together to reach the point of her opening fully to this knowing, which she will do even more so after my passing. She has no idea yet how powerful her place in this knowing will be. But she will. And it will be magnificent. Magnificent.

Charlie, I am so moved by your words, by your love and devotion toward Mary Ann, and I can deeply feel the connection you have and the reverence you share toward each other. I am saddened that you will

be leaving here, and celebrating at the same time your impending return to a peaceful wholeness. You have been such a Lightworker here, and your contributions have been appreciated by so many, and most of all by Mary Ann.

Thank you. There is no need for words about this; it is all understood beforehand [before incarnating]. It is as it should be, and I am at peace with knowing I have fulfilled my purpose.

Yes, Mary Ann has spoken to me of your beauty, your energy, your healing work, your kindness and compassion, the love you exude. You are a magnificent being, just as you see Mary Ann.

Yes, and that is why we are together. We shimmer [vibrate] the same way. It is so wonderful to dance this dance with one who knows [meaning one who understands such a connection].

To go back to what you said earlier about how you'd like assistance with your passing, Mary Ann wants you to know that she has adjusted to and is okay with your departure from this Earth plane. She does not want to in any way impede that, nor does she want you to stay one moment longer than is right for you. She does not want you to stay in your body for her sake. She loves you and wants you to be at peace, not worried about her.

I understand, and I thank her for her compassion. I will know when the moment is right, as will she. She worries about this whole process, that she won't be prepared, that she will not do the right thing, that she will miss something. Those worries will disappear at the moment my shift begins. Ask her to trust in this. And ask her to trust also that she will KNOW. She will know when the time is right. She will know what assistance to give or not give. Less is more, at least as I see it now. I do not want heroic measures and actions, I want peace and Light. Whatever will help me in that manner.

Will you be giving her any sign that you're ready to leave?

Not really. She will feel my energy winding down, even with this medicine working through my body. I will be tired, and will drift in and out of sleep. She will know. When that happens, ask her to quiet herself, listen, and accept the flow through this process. I want her to surround me with her peace and Light at that point, and be with me in Spirit as I finish up. It may not be a quick process, I don't know yet. But it will not be a heart-wrenching process either.

Thank you. Are you ready to go now?

No, but soon. It will not be that long.

Is there anything you'd like to say to Steve?

Oh, what a wonderful being HE is! He is grounded, and whole, and centered, and loving. He is Who He Is. Very clear to be around [meaning clear, balanced energy]. We have shared peaceful solitude, and roles of guardianship, and connections at a different level than Mary Ann and I [poignant feeling about male bonding, male understanding]. He is very good to, and for, and because of us. We each have flourished in this circle [Mary Ann, Steve, Toby, and Charlie]. I give my thanks to him for being there for those moments of silence, for the blending and melding of our beings, for being safe enough in himself to do that, to step fully into himself for that connection. He does not speak much of this, but he knows. He knows. And he will not forget. This connection *between us has opened his heart as well. He has suffered much loss, and he handles it with grace. I am blessed to know him.*

Thank you. And for Toby?

Ah, that one. Bless him, for he has been through fire, and dark-ness, not of his own making. And yet it was. He has seen the one side; now he sees its opposite. It is important for his journey. He has never had the First Companion position. He has been waiting behind me to do so. This will be his ultimate opportunity to shine and be Who He Is. And he will be fabulous at this. He has much time to make up for, in not having been able to share and expand that love previously [meaning his previous living situation]. *He may seem hesitant at first, but he will do just fine. We have been discussing this for some time, and he will be ready at the moment it is right for him to do this.*

Thank you. Is there anything else you'd like Mary Ann to know?

There is so much, and yet she does know. She is Love and has come so very far. I am SO proud of her. There are not words here [meaning on this planet; the language doesn't con-vey the significance] *to convey this, but I think she'll know what I mean. She is of another place, she is too gentle at times for this world* [too sensitive, as in the planet is too harsh energetically]. *But she is here to do good for many, and she is becoming Who She Is. She is close, very close. And there will come a day that she will look back and realize how very far she has come, how many layers she has shed, how much she has to offer to herself, not just to others; and how much Love is sent her way at all times by so many who hold her in high regard, both on this earthly plane and above. She IS . . . She is. All that and so much more.*

I will be with her always, no matter how many times I come together and split again. I will be with her, and she will know. It will be peaceful connections I make and symbols I send. They will bring peace to her heart and mind. There is no loss, only a shift. I will comfort her from there as I do here. She will know.

Thank you, Charlie. Is there anything else you'd like to say, or like to ask about?

Well, I could talk but it would just be words. This is enough. My messages and feelings are clear. I am tired, and ready to go soon, but want to convey my Love and good wishes and how proud I am of my beloved companions in this circle. Life here is but for a moment, and should not be wasted in struggles. But then, the struggles are part of the journey. So it is still a circle, even when it seems a straight path to nowhere. I ask that they keep that in mind when the journey seems hard. It comes back around to the Light. . . all of it is good, and right, and as it should be. And that is all I want to say.

~

I could barely read this through my tears. What a gift it was to hear Charlie's tenderness.

"Steve, here's the transcript," I said, and gingerly held it out to him. "Do you want to read it?"

"No. I can't. I can't do it," he said with a very pained look.

"Do you want me to read what he said about you? It's so sweet."

"Not now."

"Okay," I said and sat next to him. "He told Kat he's not ready to go yet. Soon, but not yet."

"Good. I mean, that he's not ready yet," he said.

"I know what you meant," I said and snuggled into him.

It would be many months before Steve was able to read the transcript.

From hearing what Charlie had to say, I felt strengthened in my trust of knowing when his time would come, though my doubt still gnawed at me. Would I really recognize the shift Charlie mentioned? Would I really know if or when he was ready for assistance?

On Charlie's thirteenth birthday, Steve and I invited friends over for a little party. For Charlie and Toby, I bought Charlie's favorite peanut butter cookies. I mushed the cookies into tiny bite-sized ones for Charlie, which he wolfed down. And Toby thought that getting two whole cookies all to himself was the best!

We adults dined on chocolate cake and vanilla ice cream and played the game of avoiding the elephant in the middle of the room—no one mentioned why we were celebrating this particular birthday of Charlie's when no previous ones had been celebrated. But the reason hung in the air like acrid cigar smoke.

Letting Go

A few days after Charlie's birthday, I perceived that his attention was more in the non-physical than the physical. Feeling that Charlie's time was near, and wanting both boys to be more relaxed, I had an animal massage therapist come and give Charlie and Toby a massage every couple of days. Along with the healings I continued to give him, I also gave Charlie daily doses of flower essences known to help with transition and surrender of death. I took the same flower essences and also gave them to Steve and Toby to help with grief.

But then I sensed a definite shift in Charlie. I felt as though it was now just a matter of days. I could feel that his Spirit was ready to go, but his body was hanging on. Yet he remained peaceful, and still enjoyed his walks. I continued to pray that he would die on his own so I wouldn't have to euthanize him. It was an enormous challenge to stay grounded enough to trust my intuition, and have faith that I would know what to do when his time came.

A few days later, I asked Kat to do another session to find out where Charlie was with the process.

Charlie, Mary Ann asked me to check in with you to see how you're doing. It's been two weeks since we spoke about your illness and how you are handling it. How are you feeling this evening?

Tired—very tired [said with a sigh; his energy feels very depressed].

Charlie, are you feeling worse than you did before she started giving you that medicine that helps take your pain away?

Well, the newness of that relief has worn off. I am still feeling pain and discomfort—not a lot, but at a dull aching never-ending level. It is draining me to hold onto this.

Hold onto the pain, you mean? Or your physical body?

Both. The pain keeps me here, as does my body. My heart and mind and Spirit are done. This journey is ended; it is time to move to the Light. But I don't know how to do that. I thought it would be a peaceful, easy, quiet shift. I am a bit frustrated that that has not happened.

I know your eye is quite different now from two weeks ago. How is that affecting you?

I feel like it's hanging out of my head. Very uncomfortable. I feel disfigured. I don't feel like this is under my control any more. [He feels he was doing well at manipulating his energy at the beginning of his illness, but now it's progressed to a point where his vital force is not able to overcome it or keep it at bay.] *And I don't like the way it's happening. I can't say that I like sitting around, waiting to die. I really thought I would just easily slip away.* [He's very depressed about this; as you mentioned, he feels this is undignified for him to have to experience.] *I am not wanting this. Not wanting this.*

Are the healing sessions still helping?

Not as before. They don't hold very long at all now.

Do you feel differently now about finding another way to leave peacefully besides under your own Spirit's power?

Well, it's starting to look more inviting [he sighs]. *I know this is not the noblest way to exit, but I can now understand why others have done so. I thought I could get through this with dignity and grace and angels singing. I'm thinking that the dignity and grace of the angels singing at the moment of my passing will happen regardless of how I pass through. So it doesn't seem as important now. I'm wondering if I'm weak-willed, if I am not the courageous being I thought I was* [he's depressed about this]. *Apparently this engineering marvel* [his body] *has other plans. I thought I could "snap my fingers and poof!" I'd be gone, with no pain and no worries. I am so surprised this hasn't happened!*

So, do you want Mary Ann's help with this?

Yes [said quietly, but clearly]. *I know she will not feel comfortable doing this, even though she says she's okay with my leaving. But who better to help me put myself to rest than the one I love so much, who loves me so much? So yes, I want help.*

Do you have a timeframe for when you'd like this to happen?

Soon. I don't want to struggle with this much longer. Not for another week or two. I see it's not going to be any easier, and it may be much harder. So I will accept assistance; there's no point in doing the other.

Anything else you'd like Mary Ann to know?

I know this will be difficult for her, but it's really not if she looks at it from the higher place [meaning spiritual rather than emotional/ego view]. *She is a kind and loving being. Sometimes it is necessary to step aside of our selves to be of assistance to others. And this is what I'm asking of her. Rather than it being a guilt and grief action, it is a kind and loving and affirming action. To help me when I can no longer help myself. To not let me struggle to get out of here. I don't want that.*

∼

After this session, I, too, was still hanging on to the hope of an easy, quiet, natural shift. I kept telling Charlie over and over that it was all right to go.

A few days later, while Charlie and Toby rested in the afterglow of their massages, I went for a bike ride. When I returned home, there was Charlie, sitting patiently and proudly inside the screen door, keeping vigil for me, like he'd done a thousand times before. My heart ripped in two as I realized that very soon he would no longer be there to wait for me or to welcome me home.

What I didn't know was that it would be the last time he would wait for me.

That night around midnight Charlie became extremely restless. After several attempts at getting him to settle down, I realized he was in a lot of pain. His potent daily dose of medicine was barely taking the edge off. I immediately gave him an additional dose. While syringing the medication into his mouth (always mixed with food to make it palatable), I could feel how desperately he wanted to leave his body, how miserably imprisoned he felt, and that the pain was keeping him trapped.

It was time to let him go. I was amazed at the tranquility with which this awareness came. It wasn't agonizing, like I'd been so afraid of. This was the "knowing" about which Charlie had explained to Kat.

~

Within minutes the medicine had taken effect and Charlie calmed down enough to lie down beside me. I did healing on him, in hopes that it might give him an easier escape route. This helped both of us relax and made me feel much more grounded. I kept telling him that it was okay to leave and assured him I would be fine. Nestled beside him, I sang all of his songs. I kissed, snuggled, and held him. I tried to stay awake, knowing it would be my last night with him. But every now and then I nodded off. Each time I woke, I lay for a few motionless seconds, afraid to check his breathing. As much as I hoped he'd die in his sleep, I didn't really want to wake up and find his dead body lying next to me. The instant I felt the slow, steady rhythm of his breathing, I was relieved. And yet, I wasn't.

During the remainder of the night I could feel the minuscule amount of attention remaining in his body. Since he was sleeping peacefully, I decided to wait until 8:30 that morning when Dr. Pat's office opened. There he could exit his body with the help of people who cared about him.

~

By 6:30 that morning Charlie was still sleeping peacefully. I marveled at the serenity that had entered me despite knowing what the next few hours would bring. Around 7:30 I woke him, took him outside for his last visit in the yard, and then gave him another dose of medicine.

I called Steve, who was in Ohio. It was the most heart-wrenching call I've ever made.

"I'm not prepared for this," he said, with a shaky voice. "But you sound so calm. I guess when the time comes, the time comes."

As I had always done when Steve was away, I held the receiver close to Charlie's ear. "I love you, Buddy!" I heard Steve say, his voice cracking. "I wish I could be there. Mom's going to take you to the vet. You'll get a shot that will make you feel better. I know you'll always be with me. We're brothers, you know."

As usual, Charlie listened intently.

Bringing the receiver back to my ear, I said, "I'm so sorry it worked out this way."

Steve struggled to talk. "Me, too. I'll call you later."

At 8:30, when Dr. Pat's office opened, I called to let them know we were coming.

As best as I could, I conveyed verbally and visually to Charlie and Toby what would happen. It never occurred to me to leave Toby at home. Toby needed to be included, to support Charlie and to say his good-byes. Of course, Charlie needed Toby there, too. What I didn't consider, at the time, was how much I would need Toby afterwards.

Before leaving for the veterinary clinic, I held Charlie on the couch for a few more minutes. It was so surreal— holding him, smelling him, feeling his velvety fur—for the last time. As I inhaled his unique, sweet smell I was overcome with gratitude, thinking of the thousands of times he had comforted me over the years. I gently kissed my favorite spots beside his nose. Then I fed him tiny pieces of his favorite peanut butter cookies, which he ate greedily. I snipped some long, curly locks from his ears and then put both boys in the car—Toby in his coveted passenger seat and Charlie in the back.

The entire way to the clinic, Charlie sat on the back seat with his rear end on the seat and his front feet resting on the hump of the floor, and gazed out all of the windows. Throughout the fifteen-minute ride, he was extremely attentive and looked at every car, tree, bird, and building we passed. He was so peaceful, and seemed grateful and proud to be watching the world one last time. Part of me wished we would enter a time warp so our time could be extended. And the other part of me felt honored to forge ahead and help Charlie enter into this new phase of his journey. I embodied a deep peace and composure unlike anything I'd experienced before.

When we pulled up to the clinic, my friend Eve, who had offered to come and lend support, was waiting for us. As a shaman, Eve's wise, loving, grounded, and Earth-Motherly nature was truly a blessing for us all.

Walking into the clinic with Charlie and Toby felt strange in its familiarity, as though we were simply arriving for a routine checkup. When we got into the lobby, Charlie even puffed up ever so slightly and scanned the room to see if there were any dogs to bark at. It just didn't seem possible that he wouldn't be walking out with us.

One of the technicians, whom we knew, met us in the lobby. "Come on in here," she gestured to a room. "Shall I get you a blanket for Charlie to lie on?"

"Thank you," I said. "I didn't even think to bring one."

Dr. Pat's associate, Dr. Emily, came in. "Let's get him settled on the blanket," she said. Then in a very warm and compassionate tone said, "Let me explain the procedure. I'll inject Charlie with a sedative, give you some time with him, and then when you're ready, let me know and I'll administer the final injection." She then turned off the lights, lit a candle, gave Charlie the sedative, and left the room.

Eve held Toby and I lay next to Charlie on the floor, quietly singing his songs in his ear.

Dr. Pat came in and knelt beside me on the floor. When I turned my puffy, tear-stained face to hers, her eyes instantly filled with tears.

"I'm so sorry, Mary Ann," she said in a whisper and gave me a hug. "Let Emily know when he's ready."

"He's ready now," I said, cradling him again.

I could feel Charlie's intense longing to be set free, to get on with his "life." I could also feel that there was only an infinitesimal thread of attention in his body. He was almost gone. Briefly, I could feel the exquisite peacefulness and aliveness of the expanded awareness he was merging into—and that *this* was who Charlie was—that he was merely stepping out of his body. And as long as I was open to feeling him in his newly expanded state, I could be with him whenever I chose.

Then I heard the door open. Dr. Emily came quietly into the room.

I put my face next to Charlie's ear and, to the tune of "You Are My Sunshine," quietly sang, "*You are my Charlie, my only Charlie. You make me happy, when skies are gray. You'll never know dear, how much I love you. My Charlie boy's the best!*"

Dr. Emily started the injection in his hind leg. Seconds later I felt a soft, gentle, but powerful *WHOOSH!* sweep through me. I looked up at Eve and feebly said, "He's gone!"

Her eyes closed, she nodded.

Behind me, I heard Dr. Emily's tender voice say, "Yes."

"OH GOD!" I wailed and buried my face in his fur.

Eve got on the floor with me and held me for a few minutes while I sobbed. Dr. Emily left the room, telling us to take as long as we needed.

A few minutes later Eve said, "Mary Ann, Toby needs you."

Toby! I'd been so absorbed with Charlie, I'd forgotten him. He was standing next to Eve looking forlorn and tentative. What a comfort it was to hold him! Thank God I had him! I could feel his sadness but could also sense his relief that Charlie was now where he wanted to be.

"At the moment Charlie left," Eve said, "I saw a triangle of light between Charlie, Toby, and you."

"I can't thank you enough, Eve."

"I wouldn't let you do this alone," she said.

I stood in the doorway looking at Charlie's body lying on the floor as if he was just taking a nap. In that moment I realized that it made no difference what I did or did not understand or believe about death. All I knew was that Charlie, in his beautiful, standard poodle body, was gone. And I didn't know how I would cope.

I thanked and said goodbye to Dr. Emily and went to the front desk to choose an urn from a little catalog for Charlie's cremains. Somehow in my emotional numbness, I remember thinking how bizarre it was to be shopping for a container that would contain the former container of Charlie.

Outside, Eve and I hugged goodbye. With Toby next to me, I looked in the window of the room where Charlie's body still lay. I watched as Dr. Emily gently folded the blanket over his body, carefully picked up his lifeless form, and carried him away. As she carried Charlie's body out of the room, the reality hit me that I would never see that body again. I put Toby in the front seat and started the car. But I didn't know where to go. I couldn't go home. I couldn't face walking in the house knowing Charlie would never be there again.

With Toby sleeping in the passenger seat, I drove aimlessly for hours. Finally, fatigued and wanting to get the inevitable over with, I headed home. Walking through the door, the emptiness punched me in the gut with such a force that I wondered if I could ever recover.

All afternoon Toby and I lay on the air mattress on the living room floor. It made me feel closer to Charlie because we had slept there for the past six weeks since it had been easier for him. Varying degrees of grief, shock, and deep, peaceful acceptance came at me in waves. I tried to flow with them all as they hit. When the prevailing undertow of grief slammed into my heart, I howled and cried. Toby just lay beside me as I held him. I felt I was crying for him too. When gentle waves of peacefulness swept over me, I felt Charlie's presence, a sweet and blissful love, a Oneness and joy-filled gratitude. I could feel him in his expanded state comforting me, telling me everything would be okay. These alternating waves of peacefulness and overwhelming grief rocked me back and forth all day.

Unlike previous times when I had grieved the loss of someone, this time I wasn't afraid of allowing myself to feel the full impact of the pain. As terrified as I'd been about losing Charlie, it was he who gave me the strength to deal with the pain of his loss.

For a few days I remained reclusive and screened every call. I appreciated people's condolences, but couldn't cope with acting brave and sounding okay for their sake.

One afternoon Toby and I ventured out for a walk around the block. A neighbor came out of her house and said, "I heard about Charlie. So are you gonna get another one?"

I was tempted to scream, "NO! It's not like a friggin' sweater!"

But aware of her good-hearted intention, I said flatly, "No, I'm not ready yet."

After this, I decided that being a recluse was preferable to falling prey to someone's good intentions. I needed a little more time to heal before facing the world again.

During these days, I twice felt Charlie's presence during the night. The first time I woke feeling the weight of a dog walking on the bed beside me. Thinking it was Toby, I looked up to see him peacefully sleeping on the floor. I knew it was a visit from Charlie. I knew he wanted to comfort me so that I would know he was still with me. I was elated to "feel" him in this way and asked him to visit again. A few nights later he did—exactly the same way. I asked him to visit again, but he never did. I was crushed and wondered why. But I sensed he didn't want me to depend on this kind of connection and was encouraging me to move on.

After Steve came back, I found him one morning sitting on the sofa, sobbing. He was holding Charlie's harness like it was a priceless treasure.

I stood quietly, gauging whether he wanted company or solace.

"Now I know how those war veterans feel," he said.

I stepped in closer.

"You know, the ones who've lost a limb. They pat their empty sleeve or pant leg in despair knowing they have to go on with their life—but they just don't know how."

Dolphin Healing

Ready to face the world again or not, some days after Charlie's death, I left Toby and Steve at home to go on a previously scheduled trip to the Bahamas to swim with wild dolphins. When I had planned the trip five months earlier, I'd been very excited about it. Then, in the weeks leading up to Charlie's death, I didn't know if I would be going. Now that I was free to go, I had no desire to. My grief was overwhelming and I wasn't sure I could enjoy anything—even frolicking dolphins. On the other hand, who better to provide healing than dolphins? The timing could be none other than God's—or Charlie's.

Sitting in Chicago's busy O'Hare airport waiting for my flight to Fort Lauderdale, I watched the throngs of other travelers and airport personnel. I wondered how many of them, like me, were enduring heartache but struggling to carry on with their lives one moment at a time, pretending that everything was okay.

Initially, the numbness of my grief didn't allow me to fully appreciate the joy of the dolphins. But their contagious, playful antics soon helped me to reconnect with myself and other people. Swimming with the dolphins, I felt their otherworldliness, which nudged me into remembering that life extends beyond this physical existence.

The dolphins' multidimensionality reminded me that I had found the answer to precisely what I had wanted to know when I began my quest—where and what Heaven is. Through it all, I had come to understand that Heaven or the Other Side is nowhere, really. It's not a "place." Ultimately I had discovered that Heaven was right where it had always been—inside me. By reconnecting with my own multidimensional, spiritual Self, I understood that the key to Heaven's door was none other than where I focused my attention.

Only now, in the muddle of my grief, I felt I had misplaced the key. But my inner experiences had given me confidence and I had learned the simplest truth of all truths—that the Kingdom of Spirit is within—and once found, can never be lost.

In one dolphin encounter, I floated on the surface and watched a dolphin circle under me. The second time it circled, I heard the clicks of its sonar and felt "unzipped" from inside out and from head to toe, as if I'd been zapped by a magic wand. A day or so later, the heaviness I'd carried around dissipated. I began to feel more like myself again—to feel alive again. I could laugh. I was on the mend.

On the last night at sea, we did a ceremony for Charlie on the back deck of the boat. With a new moon, signifying new beginnings, it was a perfect night to honor him. The air was balmy, with a slight breeze to tickle the skin. Stars shimmered across the sky and the blackness of the ocean cradled us. Our group gathered in a circle, arm in arm, swaying with the gentle rocking of the boat. As the tones of someone's chant ascended to the Heavens, I felt Charlie with me. Clasping the locks of his hair that I'd brought, I left the circle and stood at the railing of the back deck, looking out into the expansiveness of the ocean and the star-lit sky. As I held the locks of hair,

I reflected on how Charlie had cracked my heart open and that because of him, I learned that love is the key to discovering life and to understanding anything about it.

Stroking the velvety locks against my cheek, I kissed them tenderly. I stretched out my arm and released Charlie's hair to the wind, the ocean, the dolphins, and the Universe. I watched as his curls spiraled in the ocean breeze—up they went on a puff of air, and then swirled, dancing freely, down toward the ocean. As they blended with the blackness of night and were lost from sight, I remembered what Charlie had said to Kat:

I will just take a breath and float and fly away. I will be All Light, All Love, All One with that and them.

After Words

In the time after Charlie's death, I felt him often and could feel he was happy, but my grief over missing his physical presence blocked me from being able to communicate with him. I knew, however, that when the time was right, I would connect with him.

Some months later, on the same day of the month that Charlie had died, my friend Lise called, saying that she and her husband had decided it was time to have their beloved dog, Ginger, euthanized. Ginger had suffered a stroke and it was obvious to them that it was time to let her go. In connecting with Ginger and helping Lise through the heart-wrenching day, I realized that it was time for me to connect with Charlie.

Here are excerpts:

I miss you!

I'm right here! I'm with you all the time. I envelop you. So don't be so sad. Do you not see that in your deep sadness you wall off yourself from being able to feel me?

But don't I need to feel the sadness and let it move through?

Of course! But don't let it shut you out from going within to where I am!

Do you miss your body?

I miss you holding and singing to me. Will you sing to me now? You haven't sung since the day I left. [Which was ENTIRELY true—I had not sung a single note in the months since he'd been gone. I couldn't bear to. He then conveyed to me through a knowing that as I sang to him during the euthanization process, the sound vibrations created by my singing helped him leave his body.]

Were you at all afraid?

Not of the process of dying. I was only afraid for you. I know how comforting my physical form was for you. But I want you to know the comfort is still available, right here, right now— it's just not in a physical form anymore.

I feel your love at this moment—your all-encompassing, sweet, gentle love that has always filled me.

You must learn to feel that within and not rely on getting that from the physical. If you can feel it from me now, then you can still get the same love from me as when I was in a physical body. It doesn't matter that Charlie's body is no longer with you.

Tell me about where you are.

I am Here. I am now. This is all there is. You will come to know this. You will see. You will know. I am not "anywhere." I am Here. This is important! You knew me as Charlie in that Charlie body. But you didn't know ME. Now is the time to know me without that body. That body gave you comfort and much love, but remember that love and comfort came from ME! I still give you that same love and comfort. Don't turn your back to it just because you can no longer hold me in your arms. I am bigger [meaning more] *than that body you knew as Charlie. That body was only a vehicle to get your attention, pull you in to yourself. Feel me now. I am more true because without that body, I AM. Now do you understand?*

Yes. Do you miss me?

I am always here. I am you. [The understanding was that, no, he doesn't miss me because he's always with me.]

What can I do to feel you more often?

Quiet yourself. When you think you're quiet, go even deeper into the quiet. You will feel me there. Then it will get easier and easier. You knew tonight when I was here. [I had strongly felt his presence in the room, which prompted me to sit down and connect with him.]

Will you come to me in my dreams or let me feel your presence on the bed again?

These things are mere crutches. You must go deeper than that.

Is there any spiritual significance from your dying of cancer?

Only that it had to be something terminal so you could grow spiritually. It [cancer] *allowed me to finish some karma and allowed you to get back on your path of healing. Cancer is more of a modern-day disease. I had to have something of the times. Something that would help give insight to treatments* [eg. the vaccine]. *I am being healed and regenerated now. So stop trying to figure out "why cancer." Let it go.*

**What about releasing my guilt of trying to train you
with that shock collar when you were young?**

*This was also something you had to experience to help clean
the slate of the past. You didn't know any better. When I was
your horse in a past life, you used very harsh training methods
and didn't consider them harsh at the time—you didn't recognize they were harmful. This time you did. That was the
purpose. Again, it's karma working to pay off the debt. The
debt is paid. Let the guilt go now! Okay? Please!*

What is this process of returning in another body?

*It is difficult for the mind to understand. Much goes into pre-
paring a life, an incarnation. Many details must be worked
out. Everything must work together so that all can converge
at exactly the right time. It's like the past and future readying
itself to become the present. Don't try too hard to understand
it. The less you try, the more you'll understand.*

I'm not feeling as sad or separated from you now.

[I received a feeling that he was overjoyed.] *I've been waiting for you to get here.* [Meaning for me to realize I could
communicate with him. I understood he'd been waiting
with extraordinary patience for me to connect with him.]
Just don't wait so long next time. I'm here. I'm always here.

I've never loved anyone the way I loved you.

*This was meant to be so. You had to love me as you did in
order to pull yourself—propel yourself—out of yourself so
that you could know and love yourself more fully.*

I cannot begin to express my love for you. It really does go beyond this "love" thing.

Yes. Now you're beginning to get it! Love is merely a concept. Oneness of Spirit surpasses love. Oneness of Spirit IS.

Alissa Behn/Pet Personalities

Nature's message to us, I believe, is this: By embracing death in its spiritual form, we see the possibility that death may not be what we imagine it to be.

—Myron Eshowsky, *Peace with Cancer*

Resources

Brunke, Dawn Baumann. *Animal Voices: Telepathic Communication in the Web of Life*. (Rochester, VT: Bear & Company, 2002).

Ingerman, Sandra. *Welcome Home: Following Your Soul's Journey Home*. (New York: HarperCollins, 1994).

Web, Wyatt. *It's Not About the Horse: It's about Overcoming Fear and Self-Doubt*. (Carlsbad, CA: Hay House, 2003).

About the Author

Mary Ann Bumbera divides her time between farm life in North Carolina and the business world in Chicago, IL. In North Carolina she lives with her standard poodle, three other dogs, farm cats, and several horses. Visit her website at *www.BecauseOfYouIAm.com.*

Photo by Jennifer Mordini